An Anthology of Thoughts from

The Little Scribe

First published in Great Britain by UPSO Ltd in 2006

All paper used in the printing of this book has been made from wood grown in managed, sustainable forests.

ISBN13: 978-1-907172-09-0

Printed and bound in the UK
Pen Press is an imprint of Indepenpress Publishing Limited
25 Eastern Place
Brighton
BN2 1GJ
A catalogue record of this book is available from the British Library

Other titles by the author:

The Little Scribe
More Thoughts from the Little Scribe
An Anthology of Thoughts from the Little Scribe
The Pathway to Inner Thoughts from the Little Scribe
Inspirational Thoughts From Afar from the Little Scribe
Precious Thoughts from The Little Scribe
Thoughts of Comfort and Guidance from the Little Scribe

An Anthology of Thoughts from

The Little Scribe

by

Ron Bateman

A few words of explanation regarding the writings in this little volume.

In March 2000, my life-long friend and companion died, and soon afterwards I was 'prompted' to sit down and write.

What I wrote surprised me. I was 'told' via these writings that they would come from Brothers, who belong to what is known as 'The White Brotherhood'; that they would work through Brian, my companion; and that I was to be the last link in the chain as it were, for their Teachings.

I am often awakened in the early hours and I go to my study and write quickly for about an hour or so, then I go back to bed and sleep.

When I get up in the morning, I read what has been written and then record it on a cassette then I listen to, and hopefully learn from, what has been written.

I am just the scribe and can take no credit for what is written, but I feel very privileged to be part of this ongoing teaching and am very grateful to my Brothers and to Brian.

To those of you who have read this little volume, I hope the words of comfort have helped you. To those who are searching, I trust you have found what you were looking for.

May the Blessings of the One on High be with you now and always.

I dedicate this book to Brian, who is the inspiration for it, and to Irene, without whose help and encouragement this book could not have been written.

Thank you.

Ron Bateman
"The Little Scribe"

Chapter 1

REALITY OR ILLUSION?

July 2nd 2002 Morning

Yes Dear Brother in answer to your question we do wish to COMMUNICATE with you, and no it is not your imagination or thought intrusion, we are here and so we will begin our discussion with you.

You have be puzzling in your mind recently regarding not only those "spheres" that you may go to but also those other "worlds" that exist and that you may in the course of time visit and yes stay upon, not only as a visitor but also as an inhabitant!! You see dear friend, those "Worlds" or rather what you wish to term as "worlds" are a reality, just as the one that you dwell upon at present is a reality!! Meaning that it does exist and is not an illusion, though we do say that the life lived upon it can often seem like an illusion to those of inner perception like yourself!!! Though it appears as an illusion, that word does not adequately explain what it really is. For an illusion is another term for non reality, but your world is very much a reality as are those others that we have mentioned. So if you were to go to one of them it would be real and not appear as real, but in reality seem like a dream world. For all of these other dimensions are a reality and are not to be confused with your mental perceptions or shall we say your imagining's when you feel so inclined!! For often an imaginary place of existence can seem real to that part of your brain that is doing the picture making. As it does in a dream state!! For often in a dream one awakes and thinks to oneself was that real? It seemed just like it, or was it a dream? Now some dreams are a reality and that is when you have been taken to that sphere or world of perception that is devoted to the dream state!!! Does that make you wonder? For you thought that dreams are only within your own head, but that is not always so, for there is a real dream world, that does exist and to which you sometimes venture in your deep untroubled sleep state!! So that is why sometimes you revisit those places that you remember vaguely as having been to, and even lived upon!!! That may seem confusing to you but think about it and you will realize that illusion can also become a reality!!!

Well we now come, to those other planes of existence, you have wondered are you always in the "Spirit body". Well of course you are but it is NOT a Spirit body, it is one of reality and not a wraith like creature that comes and goes with the breeze. You are solid and real and yet you do have the capacity for altering your bodily tissue to suit the prevailing circumstances, but that does not mean that you are a form of what you call Spirit.

As you have so recently experienced, the other body is the real living entity and the one that you inhabit while upon the earth plane though real, is not so, for it disintegrate's if not kept alive with food and nourishment, whereas the body to which you really belong has no real need of that sort of nourishment to keep it active and alive. For on our side of life as you call it, that is the real and solid life force, and not the one that can be blown away as an illusion of reality which it never is or was!!!

We now come back to where we began, namely these other planes of perception which are nevertheless reality's!! So when you are upon them you are the same as those whose home it is and always has been! For many of these "planes" are inhabited by souls that have always been there. In other words it is their own and permanent home and it is you who would be the one who is the visitor form another plane of perception.

You see dear friend, you are the alien if that is what you wish to call yourself. You are the foreigner from a strange and unknown world, that to them seems somewhat unreal, until they get to know that the inhabitant's of that plane are real just like you are, but of a different substance, though having many of the same characteristics as those who dwell upon that world, and so you would be accepted as another form of life force.

So you can see little brother that life even as you know it does exist beyond the world that you know as home! That should be a comfort to you that reality does exist elsewhere and is not a form of illusion that you pass through when you leave behind you your body of gross material!

Material or substance exists everywhere yes everywhere whether upon your little world or the many others, seen and unseen! And just because you cannot observe them does not mean that they do not exist, for to some of those, you upon the earth are not observable to them and so if they were to be told about you, they would no doubt think that it was part of someone's fanciful imagination! And yet you are real aren't you? Just because we are not all made of the same substance does not mean that we are not real and living entities, for we all are where ever we happen to exist.

So do not think that just because you leave this world of reality that you embark upon a series of unreal lives of what you would term illusions. Far from it, little scribe, for the worlds out there and also within are very very real in every sense, it is just the way that you perceive what you see and what you come to know, for you are continually learning and observing and coming to conclusion's about what is and what is not, and that is what life is all about. It is Real, and we, that is you and all of us are real everywhere, remember that dear one. Life goes on, wherever you are, and life is for living, remember that, just because you leave one known existence does not mean that that is the end, for it is NOT it is not only a new beginning but also a continuation of the life that was given to you in the beginning. When the One on

High breathed his very breath into that slumbering body we call soul!!!

We feel that this is where we will leave you, to think upon these things at your leisure and see if they answer some of your mental questions! (that you send out to us your Brothers in Christ Consciousness. Farewell, peace be with you both and we say thank you. Farewell, Farewell, we will meet again in Thought and Reality!!!)

Chapter 2

THE VIBRATIONS

July 5th 2002 Morning

Take up your pen dear Brother for we are here to talk with you.

There are thoughts that seem to be recurring in your mind regarding those other spheres or planets that are there in the atmosphere and you wonder if they are inhabited and by whom? Can they be like us you wonder and if so what are they like and what are their dwelling places like and what are they made of? All sorts of questions that are valid if you are to get acquainted with not only those spheres but also those inhabitant's that do dwell upon them. You wonder what would happen should you one day venture upon them! Please remember that not all spheres are visible to the naked eye! But that does not mean that they do not exist for they do, but some are on a higher vibrationary force and so are not visible to you who dwell upon and are made up of lower forms of vibration! So until you can higher your own vibrations to match theirs you could not be aware of their existence, likewise they would not be able to visualise you completely you would as it were come and go and not seem very permanent to them. Every now and again they could visualise you completely and then you would fade again. So you see all forms of life force must vibrate at the correct speed when they are on a particular sphere or planet. You yourselves vibrate in unison with your surroundings, you may not be aware of this activity but nevertheless it is a positive action, and is needed if you are to be stable in your own environment!!

All life forms are made of electrical currents and if for any reason these currents are altered in any way then you feel out of sorts which is an expression of the earth people. Have you not noticed that when there are storms or high winds, some people become upset and agitated, that is because their equilibrium has been tampered with and their own electrical circuits are temporarily out of alignment! They are not physically aware of why they feel this way and if they did they would be able to rectify this out of sorts behaviour. No not by throwing a switch or suchlike but by becoming calm and less agitated by their surrounding going into a form of light coma and ceasing for awhile to be agitated. Thinking of something that will calm them down and then their whole body and Spirit can function together properly. This also goes for people that you may come across in your everyday activity.

You know yourself that when you meet someone for the first time you get what you call a " first impression". That really is your electrical frequency either gels with that person or it is out of kilter with their form of electric current and so you may feel not quite at home with them. You see we are very sensitive in our make-up and even the slightest aberration of our vibrations can cause not only distress but a feeling of being uncomfortable! So you see little brethren, there is much to learn, even about yourselves before you can attempt to learn and infiltrate others domains, and here we speak of those upon those distant spheres. One day perhaps these spheres will be able to alter their vibrations so that they and you can become as one, but that will no doubt be in the far far distant future. You yourselves will become shall we say of a lighter and higher vibration and then and only then will you be in a position to venture forth upon this quest for other civilisations and those people who make up that living force.

Now here we diverse and say that there are times when some of you can make contact with these other forms of life force, and when you ask? Well, when you leave your old earth body and transfer to the other side of life!! Where you will be vibrating at a different level. But not all persons will be able to alter their own vibrations at will. This has to be learnt by the majority of souls who inhabit our side of life! Some of you who have learnt certain lessons while still upon the earth plane will be in a position to do these things but strange as it may sound you will have not learnt these things knowingly, it is shall we say a bi-product of your way of life upon the earth, and so it is as it were an added bonus for you to enjoy.

Those who can do these things shall we say automatically will be able to not only visit these other spheres for added lessons in the way others live, but also be able to instruct as it were those whose habitation that you are visiting upon. So you see you will be helping them to understand those other life forms, as you are endeavouring to understand them!!

You can now see that the lives that await you once you transfer to the other side have wonderful opportunities for your advancement! Life goes on and is continuous but it has altered, for you have learnt how to adapt to these other circumstances and shall we say vibrationary forces. What a lot of interesting activities await those of the enquiring mind and those whose aim is to be of service!

Once you start upon this pathway, and it really starts when you are upon the earth plane, you will be able to go on to even higher things in your form of evolutionary progress. So you see little friends persevere with your studies, for they are studies. Studies in how to live in harmony not only with yourselves but with others, in fact with all that you see around you. Learn to relax, not only the body but the Spirit and the mind. Seek the solace of quietness and passivity go into that silence and replenish your very Soul and you will then feel not only refreshed, but at onement with all of God's creation.

For in the stillness of your mind you will in truth be in contact with the Spirit of the Universal Mind. The one we call our God.

We leave you here and say it has been a pleasure for us to contact you all in Thought. Peace be with you and to the little person who is doing this writing. Peace and blessings from those who you call your Brothers in Christ.

Farewell, dear friend farewell.

Chapter 3

OTHER HUMANITIES

July 7th 2002 Sunday Morning

Take up your pen little scribe, we your Brothers are here to talk with you. Do not fear, your mind is quiet and will not intrude upon our discussion. So we will begin.

You are we know anxious to find out about those other spheres or planets that exist beyond the so called Spirit Realm, which is really an inner perception of what is a real reality where we exist and have our being. We are not the same as those who dwell upon those distant spheres, the same as we are not the same as you! But are in reality a continuation of what we were when we too dwelt upon the earth plane. Though different in structure now, we were just the same as you are, and yes you to will become as we are, the same but different if you can follow our line of thought.

When you transfer from your lower sphere, you are as it were basically the same, and yet you are somewhat different in your appearance and construction, for you have developed from a gross and heavy form of matter to one of light substance, one that can be of use to you wherever you happen to be, either on this sphere or if you are "travelling" to one of the many others! Now here we digress for if for instance you were "advised" to visit upon one of the material style worlds of existence, you could; but you would not be visible to those who inhabit that plane. Do you understand what we are saying? You would be as it were a being upon that plane and yet you would not be visible to the majority of those who inhabit it, in other words to those who may be able to visualize you, you would appear in "Spirit form".

That is to say if there was a so called "medium" who was aware of the phenomena you could and would be visible to them in conscious reality and be able to converse with them in every way. For you would not appear to those gifted persons as a wraith like spirit form, but would be as solid and alive as they are!! You see they too are aware of this so called spirit world just the same as you are upon the earth, but there is a difference their own "Spirit world" is not like yours and ours!! It vibrates at a much higher and different rate than the known ones, also it is somewhat different in "construction" for it is not "ethereal" as you have been lead to believe ours is!!! Solid matter is not the prerogative of the lower planes of earth and the like. Though yours is somewhat dense and cannot be penetrated or altered at will like ours, and as those others are! Do you see what we are trying to convey to you?

Matter though "solid" can also be "transparent" when it is required to be so! That is the difference between your world and ours which incidentally will also one day be yours!!!

Other Worlds or spheres or whatever name you chose to call these other "dimensions" are all "made up" of different though somewhat similar substances. Some can be viewed, while others though real and permanent are not always visible!! It depends upon the prevailing circumstances!! Difficult for you to understand we know, just accept what we have said, for there is no way that you upon the earth plane can verify what we have stated, but it is a fact and the Truth, believe us!!!

"Worlds" that are visible to one and that does not include you upon the earth at present, need not be visible to some of the others, and yet they do exist, and so might be thought of by the "seers" on that planet as a form of "Spirit" or non-material form of life!! For to those who dwell upon those spheres and we speak of the ones that appear to be like your "world" They are of a material substance, no not the same as your earth type substance, it would appear to be of a "finer vibration" and that would imply that their form of "Earth" would be less substantial than yours, in other words not the dense form of matter that you "walk upon". Theirs would not require the heavy footfalls that take you from one place to the next! Do you follow what we are implying? They could "drift" as it were, without any physical effort, for all of their "efforts" would be effortless. You begin to wonder just what would these beings look like if their bodies are so "light" that movement is effortless! They resemble you upon earth, but of a finer substance and so would appear to your eyes (if you could see them) somewhat ethereal and "translucent" and yet to each other they are solid and of a form that is quite recognizable as what you would term "human"!!!

Now this does not apply to all forms of living matter on these other worlds of existence. It all depends on where they are in the Universe, think about that little friend. The Universe as you can see is Vast! Vast! Vast! And does not appear the same all over shall we say. There are "areas" for want of a more suitable word, that vibrate at a different rate to others, and yet they are all part of the same Universe, so you would see that those other "areas" would be different in their vibrations and so the climate would also be different !! Much for you to conjure with dear friend. For none of this can be verified by any means that you have at your disposal upon the earth plane!! What you see as the entire Universe is not the reality of it, for it "extends" shall we say beyond what you can visualize and is far more extensive than your scientific bodies realize or can even perceive!!!

In time perhaps they will be able to see "beyond" what they at present behold but that will not come about for many millenniums that the future holds!!! Remember what we have said in a previous talk, the universe is a living substance and Expands and contracts that is how it lives. Not for you to think about, we feel, it is too vast a subject for these pages!!!

We feel that you upon the earth have quite enough to think about. Ponder upon what we have given to you, think carefully and see if it makes sense to you, if not, well you haven't lost anything have you? Just a small part of your imaginative powers!!!

Farewell little scribe farewell, peace be with you and all of those upon your planet called earth!!

Chapter 4

THOUGHT

July 9th 2002 1.00 a.m.

We will begin our discussion on "Thought" and what it really means to be one who is a Thinker! You are one, and yet you do not yet know it! Thought when properly directed along the lines of Spirit communication is a wonderful achievement, for it signifies a union of "Souls" who are mentally as one!! Then Thought can be seen to be productive, for we upon the sphere of "thought" are in a unique position, for here Thought is not only everywhere, but we are Thought. You cannot quite understand that statement. For to you Thought must be the product of a mind, but in the case of the Almighty ONE. "He" is Thought and He is the instigator of all thought and that in turn in what we are, we are his very thought made manifest! A thought that starts out as an abstract being, not formed not even alive, but thought lying dormant, until, the ONE whose thought we are, breathes into us his very own Breath of life force, and so we begin our journey, a soul in search of it's maker, we travel in many spheres, until we become not just a wandering thought or being of substance, but a Thinking Entity! A product of that one on high who has not only created us but who has given us the ability to create in Thought in thoughts of love, but look around you and do you perceive even one Soul who lives up to that divine thought? You say How can we live up to what the Divine Thought expects of us for we are but frail Human beings! That my dear friend is a poor excuse for not doing what we know is right and proper. Think about that. You have had the supreme Example of Thought made Divine in the person of Jesus of Nazareth. The one who was the thought that was not only made manifest but who was and is the Divine Thought himself!! You think how can we be like him who was the one chosen by the One on High as an emissary of love and light, but then we do not have to be like Him, we can but take from his example and try to emulate his principles. Try is the operative word! God does not expect miracles, he creates them, and if you face up to life as it is, then you yourself are a miracle in the making! Just by trying to live as you know that you should and can if you really think about it. For all manifestation start's from Thought and are nourished by Thought for thought is not only Spirit but is also reality wherever one finds oneself whether upon the lower plane of thought, in other words your earth plane, or upon one of the other spheres of light that you have heard about and one day hope to inhabit.

The plane that we dwell upon is the Thought plane of mental awareness. For here all is Thought, we live by it, we create by it, we are it. As we all are! But here we learn how to manipulate thought into a positive product of love and understanding. We create in love, as the One upon High has taught us to. But it seems that it has to be learnt and learnt the hard way. When we travel to those other spheres which are not always the ones of light that you hear about, we bring to that sphere a sample of God's Thoughts of love, to lighten the darkness of the Souls that dwell upon that sphere. And when we leave we can see that what was a cloud of darkness hanging over that sphere has changed to one of light, no not the brightest of lights, but nevertheless the start of what one day will be a Beacon of light that covers the whole planet and illuminates it from not only within but without, so that it can be seen by one and all: And all of this is done by Creative Thought and with the blessing of the all Thought Creator the one we know as GOD.

You see dear friends upon the earth plane thought is a wondrous tool when used as it is intended to be, and not frittered away on idle pleasures of the body. That is abusing that gift of Thought believe us when we tell you that those thoughts are a waste of that thought substance and can only bring about disharmony. Thought is a positive tool of creativity. Use it for what it was created for, to benefit all peoples and all of the other creations that walk upon the earth that fly in the sky and that float within the oceans, for all of creation has been created by thought and needs thought to sustain its very life force! You are the custodians of Thought upon your earth plane learn to use it to not only benefit yourselves, but all those other life forms, and that also encompasses, those forms of life that grow upon your planet! You have much to think upon, another facet of that wondrous tool of Thought see to it that from these thoughts, positive actions are made manifest, and are used creatively and not destructively as we see in all parts of your war torn world! You can achieve peace and stability if you really want to. Start to build up a bank balance of pure productive Thoughts so that when they are needed they can be put to good use, for the benefit of All.

We will terminate our discourse here for we feel that you have enough to think about and work upon.

We leave you in Peace and love, and may the One on High give you the strength to carry on his work. Farewell dear little friends upon the earth farewell.

Chapter 5

THE TRUTH

July 13th 2002 12.45 a.m.

Welcome dear Brother, you were woken for a reason, and so we shall proceed to talk with you, and yes it will be the Truth that we impart, for that is what you said that awakened you. The Truth!!

The truth has many sides to it, for truth is forever ongoing and so it lives and has its form altered, but nevertheless it is still the truth. You know yourself that what is said today as a truth, can be in a few years hence looked upon, and said of it, was that the Truth? So why is it that now it has altered? No it hasn't it's man's perception of what truth is, for it has as we have said, many sides to it and we but get a glimpse of it from the angle that we are viewing it from, and as we progress so we can see more of it and what seemed like the truth before, appears now to be different, but in reality it is the same but the view of it has changed, not the truth, but how we now perceive it! And what is it that has altered our perception of that Truth? It is the fact that we have matured just a little bit further, it is called progress and what has made the difference? Circumstances? Inner thoughts? An awakening? A word that has struck a chord, and makes us sit up and notice, something, that was there all the time, but we were viewing it as if through a glass darkly, and now a light has shone upon it and we see its face just a wee bit clearer!!

Well what you say is this Truth that I should now be viewing with clearer eyes and vision? The simple answer is that you have moved up as it were and can see just that much more clearly, and that means, your inner perception has been awakened once more and you are now ready to receive another glimpse of the hidden side of the Truth!!

We talk to you of why it is that life seems so full of contradictions, you go along and then get jolted out of your happy state of tranquillity, which means that you have become used to how things are, but they are never the same, even from day to day and that is how it should be if we are to progress on the upward/inward path of knowledge and understanding.

We think we know why we are here, but do we really? We know we have revisited this earth plane to gain more knowledge, and what is this knowledge that is to fit us for our next plane of existence? Is it our everyday living experiences? Or perhaps it's how they have affected us, that is inwardly, as well as the outward vehicle that is doing the so called living! Has it shown you, just that little bit more to life than you felt when you got up in the morning? Has the day before taught you anything? Has your nighttime vigil in the world of sleep, given you an inner perception of what life is all bout? And if it has, then what are you going to do about it? Let it rest, or go ahead with a new understanding?

We may think that when we leave this vale of tears that all of a sudden everything will be made right, no more worries, no more heartaches, just everlasting bliss!! Think again my friends, you enter your next realm exactly as you have left your last one upon earth. Same, thoughts, same desires, same person as you have grown to become. Now starts a period of re-adjusting and putting into practice all those things that you have learnt, and what are they? You see them for what they really are, quite often just superficial, and of no real value to your new existence! Now, you begin to see the truth just a little clearer and so you have just learnt a very valuable lesson, you begin to see yourself as you really are, or rather how you appear to be now, but I'm afraid you are in for a shock, for the one who you thought you were has now been left behind upon that planet earth, and you are now the new being, the one that has always been hidden from earthly view! Do you recognise this new you? Do you feel comfortable with what you perceive? If you have really learnt some of the true lessons of life then you will be pleased with what you see and are!!! Now begins the start of your new round of life cycles, learning afresh, and perhaps honing what has already been learnt, for here, you are in for more learning and adapting to your new, but in some cases familiar life style, for those memories that were locked away when you incarnated upon your earth are now released, and you can see if you have learnt the lessons that you came back to learn that can now fit you for this new form of existence!!

All this may seem to you a contradiction of what you have been told about the so called "after life", but you have been some what mislead, perhaps not intentionally, even for the highest of motives, and those were to sort of recompense you for the life you have had to live while in the physical body! Do not be daunted by what we say for now you are fully awake to your new responsibilities and you learn how to cope with them, but fear not, for "time" is on your side, for here it does not matter any more, time is what you make of it, it is a "time" of learning and as we have stated, readjusting and that means not only "physically" but mentally as well you notice we say physically, for that is what we really are now, with all that that implies: You now learn how to cope with your new life and what is more important how to make it adapt to how you view it, for here it is up to you how you now wish to live!! Are you awake to your new surroundings are you ready to proceed on the next round of life's experiences? For there are many more for you to experience, and learn by.

You are now free from the bonds of the earth body, and can accomplish much if you have the "will" to do so. For you still have that choice dear friends, you are the captain of your soul, you make the decisions they are not made for you, for you are now expected to take charge of your new life and make something of it. You will be given help and guidance, if you wish to avail yourself of it, it is always there and willingly given. Not everything is just another lesson to be learnt, you are not forever being assessed either by us or by yourself!!!

The learning and living here is for your upward benefit, to help you in your evolvement into a better "human being", for you still are a human being but this time round, one of light and higher understanding! You now can "do things" with your body, that would be impossible upon the earth, here you have the freedom of "thought power", that is, once you have been taught the value of using it in the right and positive manner! Thought here is everything, it is all around you, within you, and you are "thought". Think upon that statement. "You are Thought", and that means that what you think, then you are that thought made manifest, so you can see that to be able to use thought in a constructive way, you must learn how to use it, it does not come naturally, for all your physical life you have been at the mercy of thought here "you are the master" and as the master you must be taught how to be a strict but fair master of that powerful tool "Thought Substance" for here you view the results as they are thought! So you must be careful how you think those positive actions, that result in "seen form". Much for you to dwell upon, is there not?

The life to come is one of great expectations, if you are willing to let go, of all the old ideas, and start a fresh, then this life of yours will be glorious, and full of vitality and yes service, for that is the prime lesson upon this plane of Thought. We learn to think of others first, and what we can do for them, and not what can they do for us! Though in reality when you seek to help others you are actually helping yourself and that is a lesson that should have been learnt while you resided upon the realm of earth!

We feel that this is where we will end this part of our discourse, our next one will take you further along the path of your life to come, where you will really start to live

Farewell dear friends upon the earth, Farewell and thank you little Brother with the pen, thank you!

Chapter 6

ACTION AND REACTION

July 16th 2002 Morning

Welcome dear little Brother in Christ, yes we are here to talk with you. You felt that we may wish to and you were right, so let us begin with this talk about the future lives of those who transfer from the earth plane to their new and exiting form of existence on one of the many upward/inward planes of existence!!!

We dealt before with your new entry into the world beyond your present one, here we will continue with that discourse. You have been told that you are responsible for your own actions, here and elsewhere, for even on the earth plane, you know that, what you do has a "knock on" effect to those around you as well as to yourself. For every action has a reaction, whether it be good or the reverse. You notice we do not say "bad" for most everyday actions do not warrant that word. Though there are times when what was a good intention sometimes ends up as the reverse, so you see there is much to contend with even upon your earth isn't there?

Now you begin to see that actions taken upon that sphere can and do have repercussions upon the next one!! You cannot escape the results of your premeditated actions! Think upon that, we have said "premeditated" and that should tell you what we mean. The "ordinary" shall we say actions do not usually result in lasting "reactions" and can somewhat be discounted. It is those others that you must consciously think about, for they are the ones that are impregnated upon this other sphere that you will one day gravitate to, so you must begin to "store up" for yourself positive good reactions and not negative ones for it is those that will take a long time to dissipate and will somewhat "hold you back" in your new progression! We are trying to impress upon you all, that actions whether positive or negative, all have their opposite counterpart and so must be learnt how to negate negative from the positive, and in time if you are wise, you will make the positive, the real positive, one so that it becomes the normal mode of living, for remember you do not leave those results behind you when you leave your earth body, for they await you when you arrive here and must be accounted for!!

Now we go forward and assume that all those debts have been paid, and the good ones are now ready to speed you on your journey. Where will that take you, you wonder? Once you have shall we say "settled in" then you are shown various avenues of "work experience" that can help you on your evolutionary path upon this particular sphere. You are not pushed into any particular plan of action, you see the results before they even happen, and then it is up to you to chose the one that you think is the correct one for you to impart upon!!

This is also a learning sphere like all of them are, only as we progress "higher" then the learning becomes less and less for we are now living what has been learnt in the past and so progress is more rapid towards the ultimate goal of perfection! But that will not come about for many, many, life times hence! So we will leave that part now and continue with what will now be your "present existence". You will have renewed your acquaintance with those of "like minded" experiences, some from the past and some that are now in the future, which is the Now!! Life has now opened up new vista's and new horizons, things to tackle and make you use your little grey cells, oh yes you still have them but not quite the same as before! Here your thinking takes on not only a positive action but also a "physical" one, in other words what you have thought, it now IS!! A product that can be seen and used if so desired! This thought form that you can now use is a valuable tool in your new existence and must be used wisely, so before you embark upon this new round of experiences you must be taught how thought is to be used for productive and positive work and not negative, as some of our pupils tend to use it mainly for their own amusement, but thankfully this phase soon passes when they see what other's can achieve when thought is used as it is intended to be!!!

No, this is not all "hard work", you now have the capacity for thinking properly and so to learn new skill's will be a joy and not a burden!! You are shown by example just what thought can accomplish and that will inspire you to try and emulate what your teachers have shown you. You may think, does that mean we have to sit in a classroom? Back to childhood again?! No, dear friends for the "classroom" is life itself if you can follow what we are saying! You will be encouraged to see this new found function of creative thought to not only help yourself, but also whose who are not so fortunate as yourself! You see dear friends, life here is not so different as it was when you dwelt upon earth. There are still hurdles to climb over, and the fastest way to do that is in service to those others who are in need of it. Do not think that just because you are now in the next world or plane of existence, that all is honey and light, it is not, for as we have pointed out in our previous discourse, when you awaken on our plane of existence you are virtually the same person as you have always been and for some that is a great shock, for they now see themselves as they really are, warts and all!!! No amount of disguise can alter the fact, and so you see, there are always those who need a "helping hand" to help them in their onward progress. Think about that, for is that not a worth while occupation? To bring a soul out of the darkness of misunderstanding and into the light of God's healing love, which is what we, you, all of us, are capable of giving to one another!! That my friends is only one of the many options that are open to you to explore and see if that is what you feel you are capable of doing.

Life upon the other spheres is for ever ongoing it never stands still and yet you are not expected to be forever tending to others needs. You are free to do what you wish, within reason of course! For remember that even here as elsewhere, there are rules and regulations that are put into place for your benefit as well as others!! Abide by them and life is wonderful, flout them and you will suffer the consequences!! Brought about by your own selfish actions!

There, we would like to tell you about all the wonderful places for you to visit to enjoy as you've never been able to before, no, tiredness, no hassle just freedom to explore at your leisure and your own pace, with those who you wish to associate with, but we will leave that for another time!! So for now we will leave you in Peace and Harmony and may the Blessings of the ONE on HIGH be with you now, and for always. Farewell dear friends and little scribe upon the earth plane. Farewell.

Chapter 7

POSITIVE THOUGHT

July 18th 2002 1.45 a.m.

We begin our discourse where we left off, namely, the next world and those who dwell upon it, for it is a place of habitation, a reality in every sense of the word. This world is your next one on your spiral of evolution. This is the stepping stone to the realms of eternity. You have now made the first step, and there is no turning back,. This is theoretical, for you are still dwelling on the earth plane, but this is what awaits you, when you transfer to our plane of existence, though in reality this next "world" is not our permanent dwelling place, we have as it were "moved on" but we return to instruct and advise, all part of our life's pattern of teaching.

You wonder what this new life of yours holds for you? Well it holds the key, to unlock your inner being from it's shell of dense matter, and so you can start to readjust yourself to these surroundings of light and thought transference, for this world is your entry to a new phase in your evolutionary lifestyle!! You have been told before about the substance of Thought, that you are taught how to use, and use constructively, here, thought is paramount, nothing but nothing can be accomplished without it!

You will be amazed at just what it is that thought when properly used, can accomplish! What you see and perceive when you enter our world is the true reality of life, yours has been transient and somewhat "illusory" a reality yes, but only in as much as it has sustained your life force while inhabiting the earth plane, but it is a form of illusion, for it is not a permanent dwelling place, it is sustained by thought and that from the Almighty for as long as He deems it is necessary, and when it has done what has been required of it, it will disappear, back into the Eternal chaos of creativity!

This of course is not something that will happen for a very very long time, but it is inevitable for your world is somewhat unstable in it's makeup and subject to many laws of limitations, not like the one to which you will next travel to, and yes, live upon.

This world is "permanent" and will not "disappear " though it too can be altered and adjusted to keep pace with the new surroundings. You see nothing stands still in the overall scheme of the ONE on High. Life in all its aspects is one of constant change, but that does not mean that it is not "permanent" it all depends on how you view where you are, with your inner perception!!! This is a realm of re-awakening to your new life and responsibilities, wherever you find yourselves dwelling. You are part of the whole fabric of where you dwell!! And so you must learn to live in Harmony not only with one another but also with your immediate surroundings, for as you are part of them so you affect your immediate locality, do you follow what we are saying? Here you do not just exist as it were, you now see just what life here has to offer you, it may seem somewhat strange at first when you find that this new found freedom is not just an illusion of the mind!! For upon earth you have been limited by your laws of that plane, the denseness of it has been a restriction, hampering your potential, here, the freedom that you now experience, will prepare you for your future development! You do not stand still, here for all is life and that means living in every sense. You are here for a purpose, you have shed your earthly garment and now you are in the one of translucent light, though still resembling your earth body, but with no restrictions that that one is heir to!

You are now fully awake and can start to progress in what is now your only life worth thinking about. For it now goes on and on, never stopping, you are here to further your progression ever upwards! Though that should not be taken literally, for this expression "upward" is really another word for inner understanding and perception. Your new freedom will bring you into contact with not only being's of like substance and outlook, but also beings of light from those planes of inner knowledge and understanding, they are not only your teachers but also your friends whose job it is to guide you in your new life style!! Do not feel that you are going to be restricted by what we have said. It is all up to you, no one forces you to do anything, you see by example, and then you too wish to emulate what it is you have perceived, now you are ready to be shown how best you can start to live, not only for yourself but for others also!!

This is how you should have lived while upon the earthplane, but sadly it seems that the form of competition that pervades that plane, hampers your innate desire to help others, you see them as something of a threat to your own advancement. While here there is no friction of that sort, you do not have an axe to grind you are past that stage forever.

Service and the love of your fellow man is what we hope to show you works for that is what all life is about, for that is how we all progress! Do not feel that all of life is one long round of searching out different ways of helping each, other, for we all have to learn how to stand upon our own two feet do we not? Though that metaphor is somewhat ambiguous, for here standing on ones own two feet, does not actually apply, if you can get our inner meaning!!! Freedom of movement is one of the many many joys that await you here, for the waves of thought can take you wherever you wish to go! You have much to explore and enjoy once you have adapted to your new surroundings. You will no doubt wish to avail yourself of all of the delights that are at your disposal and once you have "got over" this initial taste for adventure then you can start to live your new life as it should be lived! And that is for the benefit of all, that is all around you, for you are now a part and a very necessary part of the fabric of this new world of yours.

As a "world" you will want to know what it consists of don't you? Cities, continents, towns even hamlets for not all people wish to live in the city you see life has moved on and yet it can appear as the same as the one you have just left behind. But it is different make no mistake about that. You are what you think here, and that also goes for your surroundings! That makes you think about it, what would you do with a palace? There's more to life than opulence for opulence sake isn't there? You learn to inhabit what you know is suitable for you and not just a fanciful edifice, which you would tire of very shortly believe me. We have all gone through that phase and believe us when we say that some of the so called dwelling places that have been created by thought are nothing but empty shells that crumble and disappear as soon as they are created! To create a substantial and permanent dwelling abode, needs careful and productive thought and you have to be taught the right procedure before you can attempt anything on that scale!!

Thought though limitless has its laws that have to be adhered too if you are to make this life of yours productive and worthwhile! Think about that dear friends upon the earth. Nothing comes easily, it all needs effort and Thought the most important word that you will ever come across! And we say Think about that and come to the right conclusion. So much can be accomplished with positive and regulated thought.

We feel that this is a good time to bring to an end this part of our discussions on the life that awaits you once you have left your earthbody behind you!! You no doubt want to be told more of what awaits you, you will be in "time" and so we bid you farewell, think carefully about what has been given to you, it is not fanciful illusion, but true reality.

Start preparing yourselves for the life to come, alter your outworn thoughts, think afresh, do not be backward in looking to the future, for that is where your true life lies!!

Farewell little friends upon the earth farewell to you too little Brother, Farewell.

Chapter 8

WHAT IS TRUTH?

July 20th 2002 3.20 a.m.

We begin our nights discourse with the words "What is Truth". Truth is such a strong word and is so often misrepresented, for truth to one can be an untruth to another. So often a truth once stated is somewhat difficult to understand or appreciated, for one feels that if one starts to try and unravel a truth then one may find oneself at a disadvantage for one may then perceive another facet of the truth that one was completely unaware of and so in one's mind one begins to doubt! Here we are speaking of the truth of the Divine, not the mundane ones of everyday living!!

You will ask, what we mean by Truth's of the Divine? How can we possibly know them or even understand them if shown them? A good question, for even we wonder at times what is and what is not the Truth! We speak here of what we poor mortals try in our own feeble way to try and unravel what should be obvious but each time we think ah! This must be the truth, we find that round the corner lies another facet of that illusive form of truth and what it is trying to tell us!!

Now if we say to you, well the basic truth is this, and then give you a lengthy explanation of what we see as the truth, you will either have to take our word for it, or think to yourself, can that really be the truth, and then that sets up a conflict within your mind, so how are we to combat this form of shall we say mistrust of what is said but cannot be verified by human understanding? Should we, that is you we are talking about, just accept what is given and not even question? That we feel is what you would term Faith, or should you question what has been said and try to work it out for yourself? That we feel is the correct way to enhance your knowledge and understanding and in doing so you are beginning to not only perceive but understand what has been imparted to you. Now all this talk you will say has got you nowhere, but has it dear friend? It has started you thinking has it not? And that is what this nights discourse is all about. For you to think, now shall we give to you a facet of the Truth that you have not been shown before? Or have you just forgotten and put what you thought aside, in your everyday living? For life requires much of your mental energy to cope with it, and leaves precious little time to sit quietly and try to understand the underlying principles of what life really is for?

And what is it for? Why to live as Christ showed us how to, with love and compassion for all of humanity and that includes not only mankind but also all of the life forms that inhabit your world of earth!! Love is the main Truth, if only we could live up to it, for to truly love in the Universal sense is to give oneself wholly to that principal, without reservation. That means, thinking of others, and how your whole attitude affects them. When love in those terms is expressed how it is intended to be, then we can really begin to live a Christ like life, to prepare ourselves for the true life to come!! The whole of this life upon earth is to try and teach mankind the real reason for his being upon this planet. It is to try and prepare him for his everlasting life to come when he eventually leaves his struggle upon this earth and leaves behind the body to which he has been using as a form of habitation and puts on his true garment of celestial light, which does not mean, that once he has left the earth he is fitted to become an angel of light!!!

Many more life times upon the upward spheres are needed before he can feel he could be called that, and even then he would not really be an angel, for angels are not made of human material, they are translucent being's of pure thought and so emanate a light so brilliant that you could not perceive them with your naked eyes, but only with your inner perception!! So, cease your wondering on that score, you start out as an human embryo and that you will remain, shall we say basically, for you will change as you get higher, in understanding and knowledge so that your being becomes, "light" not from without but from within, which in turn radiates your whole form with its own luminosity!!! Much for you to try and think about. You will ask, how do we become this luminous being that you say we will become eventually? The answer is simple live in love and Truth for love is the answer that we all have to seek and put into practice if we are to become what God intended us to be! A symbol of his Divine love made manifest for all to see!!

And how can we do this? By surrendering self to Him and that means doing unto others what you would wish them to do to you and that is unselfish love in all you do! It sounds so easy and yet so difficult to put into practice it seems. For we are all individuals and that means that we feel we must look after self first, but that is not what God has created us for, it is to show love and compassion in selfless acts of kindness to all of his creations, then and only then will we be able to see the true nature of what is termed Universal love if Mankind could but see that that is the only way for him to live upon your earth in complete harmony with all things and that includes Nature which is the Mother of all!!! Start to try and live up to the principles that were given to us oh, so long ago, and have been by so many of earth's example's of what Man can be when he learns to put self behind him and seeks to try and live for others, and that will in turn include himself for in loosing himself in service he finds his true self and that is the God within. Think upon this truth for it really is the Truth. We all are a part of that Divine principle known to all as God the Creator for He has created in pure love and that means His love is unselfish for He has given us the freedom of will, to either live for

Him and by Him or live for oneself, and what will that achieve? Not satisfaction for sure. So start to readjust your lives, put aside this thought of Me and me only and think of other's and in doing that you are thinking of God and behaving as God wishe's for after all He is our Father and Creator and so we are all a part of Him, and so are endowed with His attributes however small they may be, they are the essence of His love.

We leave you here with those words His love and that is the whole Truth that man is forever searching for, and yet it lies within him all the time. Peace be upon you dear friend's!! and upon the little one, peace and again we say peace.

Chapter 9

THE GOD WITHIN

July 22nd 2002 1.00 a.m.

Jesus the Christ, We speak to you in His Name for the Christ Consciousness dwells within us all, and always has been there. Given by God our Father and creator. For in truth the Christ within is that part of God that He has given with His Love to promote the understanding of why it is that we are upon this planet in the first place. But dear friends do not think that you, that is the Mankind who dwells here is the only species that has been endowed with this internal vision of the Christ spirit. For that spirit or shall we say that awareness, is within all of the Human species, and you have read that correctly for we are all Human regardless of where it is that we dwell in the Universe! For the Christ Spirit is our conscience made manifest!! You thought that what we call our conscience was just another name for our perception of what is right and what is wrong. Well that is so, but it also has another name, and that name is Christ Consciousness, for without it we cannot hope to know God.

Seek your inner state of awareness and you will find all the treasures of the universe, there within you and what is this treasure that we speak of? It is the essence of the Almighty that dwells therein, lying as it were dormant, waiting for that spark of Christ consciousness to bring it to realization of who we really are, and that is? Children of the one and only Father, the one we call our

God! He is Universal in every sense. He does NOT belong to just one sect or creed, or Nation or one particular culture He is boundless and that means He is everywhere and in everything that lives for it lives because of His Breath the Breath of Selfless love, that sends forth His offspring on the pathway of inner knowledge of right and wrong of good and bad, of love and hate. We are made up of all of these so called qualities, for all things are made up of Negative and Positive vibrations, each needing the other to exist, but, they must eventually come together as one, and that one is the Positive Good, which is another word for GOD.

We are created from his very being and so we are fundamentally the Good part of GOD, not knowing who and what we are, it is only when we are estranged from him that we begin to realize just what it is that has made us who and what we are. When we have awakened to that knowledge then we can begin our journey back to where the Creator is waiting for his creations to return to the Source of all Creation! Will we ever reach that goal? That is something that will never be revealed to us until we are there, but that does not mean that we cannot strive towards it, even if we never actually "see" where it is that we are heading for.

You may say, if we are not allowed that view until it is as it were too late, what is the point of all of this striving? Well the point dear friend is the ultimate union with the ONE on High, the ONE and only God of this our Universe!!

Life has been given to us to explore "ourselves" to try and get a glimpse of that part of us that knows itself as part of God. Many of us do not even think along those lines, for when we do then it is that we have begun to "grow up" and take our rightful place among all of God's creations. As part's of the living God it is our duty to try and behave as we know how we should loving one another, and seeing in each other that Divine spark that joins us all in the Brotherhood of Mankind. Look not upon the colour of a man's skin, but look within that outer covering and see that spark that dwells within that body and know that you too have that same spark of the Divinity within you as well, and so your brother is your neighbour and your neighbour is in reality your Brother!!! That also goes for all of those other forms of Humanities that are at present unknown to you upon this earth plane! Yours is not the only lived upon planet and think not in terms of what you think you see with your eyes! For there is more to Heaven and Earth than you can ever visualize with those fiery orbs, that you see with, and yet do not see with what is the all seeing eye, the one within!!!

Understand yourself, analyse what it is you perceive, are you the God like creature that you think you are capable of being? Or are you a travesty of the one on High? It is all up to you, for within you is the blueprint of what you are capable of becoming, you have all of the components that go to make up a creature of God like substance. Release that substance that lies dormant, and start to live as you know you should! Live for one another, for in doing that you are doing the work of the Almighty, be at peace not only with each other but also within yourself. Accept that you are part of God and start to behave like one! For after all we will all one day return to our Father in Heaven and what will we be able to show Him? That we are a part of Him and so like Him? Or will He find us wanting? Start now to live in the manner that you know is the right one, seek not to preen yourself for you are all the same underneath, it is only this outward shell that makes you think you are different. Love one another that is all that God asks of you, He created you in love, return it to Him by living in Harmony with all of creation. That is the lesson that we have been put upon this sphere to learn and live by. Love that is the answer to all of life's problems if only we can accept that principle.

Live in love and love to live, for that is all that there is to know. We leave you in Peace and Love, we bring that to you in all humility. Peace be with you all.

Farewell little Brethren of the earth Farewell, Farewell!

Chapter 10

THE CHRIST WITHIN

July 24th 2002 1.15 a.m.

Dear Brother in Christ Consciousness. It is in His name that we greet you, little scribe put aside your thoughts and let your pen do the work.

Here we will begin this nights discourse. We speak of Christ and then think that encompasses all we have to say on the matter, but indeed it is not for the word "Christ" is a powerful word when used in its right context. The Christ Consciousness, was manifest not only two thousand years ago, but even before that period in man's history and believe us when we say to you is still alive and active in this your present day.!!!

The Christ and we shall still say the "Christ Consciousness" for it is a state of "mind" and not just a perception of what has been taught you all these years. For that consciousness is indeed a living breathing consciousness that dwells within each and every one that is what you term a living entity and that if you care to think about it embodies not only you upon this earth plane but also on the many other spheres of existence and perception this "spirit" which is another term for what God in His wisdom has endowed us with is what will bring us back into his arms once more, for we have strayed far from His original conception of us, and yet that is what was planed, a paradox you say, how can God bring us back when it was He, who sent us forth in the first place?!!!

You are aware we know the reason that we were put upon the path of knowledge and understanding which in the original form was and still is unknown to most people's. Though today there is an upsurgence in thought why it is we are upon this planet of earth. Man is making strong efforts to see if he is alone in this universe or if by chance there are other life forms that not only resemble him, but can also be contacted. You will no doubt wonder, if then there are other life forms that resemble mankind is that Christ spirit also within them and if so how did it get there, when Mankind seems to think that that Spirit belongs exclusively to him and him alone. Not so, dear friends, for if the one on High is the Creator of "All Life" then that Spirit must inevitably reside in all of those other creations as well as within your own. But do not think that what we have said is the end of this subject, far from it, for if that consciousness is universal (which it is!!) then all of the "humanities" are from the one and only source of creation. You have had your Masters and teachers through the ages, and all of them have been imbued with that Spirit of Christ, do not confuse the Christos with the Man whose body was taken over literally by that force!

All ages have their "Christ's" but are not perceived as such until they have long departed from the earth plane and then they are recognised for what they were and what they achieved, one day perhaps you people of the earth will be able to recognise a Christ Spirit when it dwells amongst you, and when you start to realize that, then you will know that you truly are on the upward path back to the Almighty One we call our Heavenly Father! Think upon that, we say "Heavenly Father" and leave it at that but that is a mistake for our Father does not dwell in some far off land somewhere upon a sphere that we call "Heaven" , He is everywhere and is within everything and everyone, regardless of how they may appear to the human eye!!! Do you understand what we are implying? We tell you that the Christ Consciousness which is the God within reaches out to not only your world but all those others that you seek to find and sometime wish to dwell upon. But think again little people of the earth, these other spheres of existence also have their inhabitants, and perhaps would not look kindly of an invasion from one of the lower spheres of existence. If as you think you are not the only species of the humanities then you must understand that their territory is theirs and not yours to venture upon without their consent!! Have you thought about that? Or in your arrogance you think you have a right to trespass upon others domain without first seeking their permission!!

Study the Heavenly bodies carefully and not only with the naked eye but with the inner perception, use that Christ Consciousness to govern your actions, use it to alter your desires for global transgression, search your own hearts first, make of your earth a safe dwelling place, before you try to explore those other spheres that you seem bent on discovering, for perhaps they do not wish to be discovered by what they perceive are a backward race of human like beings!!! Think upon that, for the life forms that you seek to discover are not so far from you as you think, it is just that you are not yet in a position to discover them with your present outlook on what other humanities may be like!! Vibration is what we are talking about!! We feel that until you can not only understand that but actually embody it and that means live by it, you will not be able to perceive what it is that you are seeking! But remember that as we have said, The Christ spirit or consciousness dwells within all and so though you are at present alienated from those other forms of life, you are in actuality part of them! Joined as it were by that inner force of God understanding that He has given to us all. They are not only your Brothers in Christ Consciousness but they are also your nearest and dearest if you did but know it. That thread of the Divinity binds us all together, like a golden chain, a chain of pure love and understanding. Understand yourselves first, and then and then only seek to understand and acknowledge your Brother's in Christ that dwell upon those other sphere's that are at present unknown to you!!!

Accept that God is not only on your doorstep but is also all around the known, and also the unknown and unseen areas of your Cosmos. There is life in abundance out there. One day you may all come together and then the Creation of the Almighty will have reached it's conclusion and then what? It is not for us to speculate on that for that is in the far, far, distant future and perhaps may not come about how we may envisage!!

We return to our main theme the "Christ Consciousness" look within, seek it out, for it does dwell within you, yes even within this earth shell that you inhabit while upon this lower sphere, for that Consciousness is the real reason for you being alive in the first place. Awake to yourselves, seek first that spark of the Divinity that it the real you the one that must eventually return to its source! The source of all creations. Remember the man Jesus was and is a symbol of what mankind can become, for he is the universal blueprint for the Brotherhood of All mankind's!! Think upon that word, MANKINDS that should tell you that we are speaking not only of your earth plane but of all those others seen and unseen, known and unknown, but they are realities.

You are not alone in having your Christ's for there are many if you did but realize it, but they do not all go under the same name and are not all of the same colour, race, or what you term creed!! Think upon that, you have for too long isolated yourselves within your so called religious cultures, when in reality you are all the same, it all depends on your outlook of how you perceive the Creator be He God, Allah, Jehovah, or one of the many other names that you call the one who is NAMELESS. We are all part of that one that we have called nameless and so we are all of the same form of life force, and so we are all ONE. Think upon that before you gaze upon another person with a jaundiced eye of distrust and even hatred, we are all of the same family of humanities, behave as God has intended you too, different but alike! Look with love upon your neighbour and seek that Christ Spirit that dwells within us all and know that in truth we are all ONE.

We bid you farewell dear Brethren of the earth, much for you to think upon and act upon also. Peace be within you and help you to release that Spirit of Christ Consciousness that is there waiting to be released.

Farewell, and farewell little scribe and Brother farewell.

Chapter 11

LOOK WITHIN

July 28th 2002 Sunday Morning

Peace be with you dear little Brother, peace and blessing from the One on High.

Once again we use your pen and we thank you for this opportunity to converse with you.

We will talk to you about the one you call Jesus The man from God who walked your earth two thousand years ago and yes still does, no dear one not the man but the Christ Spirit that dwelt within, for that brief span, that has in fact shaped humanity, for his teachings have become universal in more ways than you can ever imagine. For the Christ Consciousness is that part of the Almighty that He has allowed us to be imbued with, in the understanding that it is used for the better understanding of all those other forms of living matter. Man so often thinks that it is he who is the important creation of the One on High he may think along those lines but believe us, he is not the only creation that warrants the title of Man. Think about that and you will realize that Man as such is one of many not only those who you see around you, but also those others that so far are unseen by you upon the earth!!!

Man is made up as it were of many facets, and all of them go to make up the Soul of Man for he is not what he observes when looking upon his face in the glass of reflection. The one that is reflected is but an illusion given as it were as a guide to what is really hidden from the outside view! Man is complex, and until he understands the many facets that go to make him up he will never be satisfied. And yet that is what he is all about, finding out just who he is not the one he sees but the one that he knows dwells somewhere not in this earthly body, but one upon a distant sphere, waiting for the reunion with that part of himself that he allowed to be incarnated upon the lower sphere called earth!! Look carefully within that shell, when you seek your solitude, when you try to commune with the Spirit of God, which is your own higher self if you did but know it. We are all a part of that Divine being that we term God, we are not only His children but we are also a living part of His very essence and so we must try to emulate that spark that has been given to us, and what is that spark? It is the Christ Consciousness that we have spoken to you about.

It is that part of the Divinity that is present in all of us. It comes as it were when we are ready to receive it!! We are not born with it even though we have the potential, there waiting to be awakened to its true purpose. Jesus the Man was and still is the supreme example of what Man and that encompasses all of the Humanities can become when he open's himself to the Divine Spirit that dwells within him, but is so often pushed aside in Man's attempt to further his own physical development, by which we mean his selfish desire to promote his physical vehicle along the path of material advancement. Man can advance, but need not trample other's in the doing so. That is a prime lesson for him to learn. Seek not the selfish road in life for it only ends in disappointment and disillusion and where does it all end? Why when the body ceases it's breath and enters its new life, and what will it take with it? Certainly not any material possessions, for they remain upon the earth, while the treasure's of the Spirit are carried over and how will they fare when viewed against all the other attributes of the new but old form of living matter that you call a body!!! Which there again is but a covering for what dwells within.

Have the lessons been learnt while you tarried upon the earth plane? You now have time for reflection before you can begin your new round of learning and experiencing. Will that reflection and subsequent re-adjusting be long or short? It all depends on you and your outlook, for though you are now in your new environment you still carry with you baggage from your previous life!! Will that be a heavy load to carry or will it be light, a small pack on the back that you can carry with ease?!!!

You have come a long way to enter this new phase of your existence which will we hope be your now permanent one on the upward spiral back to the source of All creation. You should now be fitted and ready for this journey. No looking back and no regrets, for the life ahead is one of pure joy, though that does not mean that it will not require effort, for life does go on, it hasn't stopped because you have just left that lower dimension. You will still have challenges to overcome and profit by, all to prepare you for the next stage in your evolution, the journey is there for you to embark upon with your new found freedom of travel and we are speaking here of the mind and not the present vehicle you will be inhabiting! A lot for you to learn and try to understand. Be a true child of God the Father, and act as you know He would wish you too, and that means, studying others and not just yourself. Remember you aren't any different from when you resided upon earth, same thoughts and desires, except that now you are in a position to use them as they should be used and that mean's not selfishly!!! There is still plenty for you to do and learn in this new life of yours, see to it that it is a profitable one and one that speeds you on that upward path. Release the Spirit of Christ within you, let it be your guiding force, for it is the one that will take you, back to where you long to be.

Peace and Blessing's be upon you dear Brethren of the earth!! And peace dwell within you little Brother. Peace!

Chapter 12

THOUGHT ILLUSION

July 31st 2002 2.30 a.m.

Take up your pen Little Brother in Christ Consciousness. We your Brothers are here to converse with you.

You are here to be informed of what it is that will await you when you transfer to our plane of Thought, for indeed it is a plane of Thoughts, but that does not mean a plane of endless pleasure of thinking what shall I do next!! Our plane or rather the one we are on at present though it is not our permanent dwelling abode. This plane of Thought is for the newly arrived as it were, Souls who are on the upward progressive journey back to the Source of all Creation! When you first come to be awakened to your new surroundings you begin to wonder just where you are and why it is all so familiar. There are various reasons, some are that you have dwelt upon this plane of Thought many times before and so are familiar with your surroundings, another reason is that all the buildings and locations are familiar to your senses, and you notice we have said senses! That should give you a clue as to what we are implying for your senses are now heightened to a high degree. You see things not as they are but how they appear to be to you and you alone!! Difficult for you to grasp. For this plane is a plane not only of thought but of thought illusion!! Think about that little Brother. "Thought illusion" that is exactly how it is!!! All appears to be real, solid, and just as you imagine but in reality it is not what you think you perceive. It is all done as it were to reassure your mind senses that you are now in a familiar World of reality, for this world is a real one, make no mistake about that, but it is one of endless possibilities for the advancement of the mind intellect. That is what we upon this plane are all about. We are here to stimulate your Thoughts process, to let you see just what you are capable of becoming once you have adjusted yourself to your new environment.

Here all is a form of changing shapes and idea's you notice that we have said ideas for that is very important, for all things start from a thought of an idea, be it spiritual or what you can call material, or if you wish physical, for yes even here we do appear and are physical to the human eye, for believe us you still are a from of human being like substance, but and here we stress the point, human like substance read that over and digest the meaning. Substance is a form of energy that can be manipulated and not only formed but observed as a reality, though in actual fact it is but a thought illusion!!!

On this plane which is one of many you are taught that all is not what it seems!! Thoughts change and so do the surroundings that you inhabit, but that does not mean that for the time being they are not a positive reality to you. Think upon that To You and if you are following our line of thought you will know what we have said!!! Once you have grasped this concept of what is real and what is not then you can begin your next phase in your upward progress. So you see little friend you have much to learn, even though you have been thinking what else is there to learn that I haven't already understood!!!

Here you will be shown how you can cast aside all your outgrown ideas and thoughts of what this your next phase of life is all about! Though it all looks familiar, and as you now understand, it is for a reason, its for you to adjust carefully to what this new experience has to offer you, to help you to grow in stature and that means the mind!!! You are not expected to take it "all in" at once, there is a long period of adjusting, though in reality it takes no time at all, for time here is but another form of illusion!!! This world though like your old one, is not the same in any way whatsoever!! Once you become adjusted to this new way of observing things around you then you can start to open up the avenues of new experience to begin to live as we do, while we tarry upon this to us a lower sphere. You see dear friend we have progressed not only to the next sphere of perception but even higher than that one, but this coming down as it were, is all part of our teaching syndrome, for we are Teacher's of light and understanding and what we have been taught we pass on to those who have the ability to understand and comprehend just what it is that they are here for!!

Not all souls and we use that term loosely, not all souls wish to be shown the ins and outs of their new found existence, they are quite content to remain in this state of permanent illusion!! One day they will tire of the excitement of it all, and then they too will seek the inner knowledge of what life is all about, but until that time comes, we respect their desire to remain as it were in sublime ignorance of what is reality and what is not!! Much for you to conjure with is there not little friend upon the sphere of earth? But this discourse should open up your mind to the possibilities of the future. It is one of glorious awakening. No longer will you be fumbling in the darkness of doubt, for you will now be in the light of understanding and inner knowledge.

Your real schooling has just began, look forward to a lifetime of education and upliftment where all things are possible to those whose minds are open and whose hearts are full of God's love! The lives and we do stress that word the lives to come are full not only of promise but of promises fulfilled through effort and love always remember that, through effort and love. You are doing God's work, and that should encourage you to respond in the only way that is possible and that is with loving service to all around you.

Here you are to be shown just what you are capable of becoming, in the service of our true God and master. Though do not read that word in it's earth bound connotation, for Master here means something quite quite different! You will know the true meaning in due course!

When you have finished your living upon this sphere of intuition and upliftment you will be ready to become a probationary co-worker with the One on High as we all are to start with, so do not look aghast at what has been written. On probation means that you as a willing subject are being helped along the way to enlightenment, and are viewed as to how you are progressing. This takes a form of mutual understanding and not examinations as you might imagine!! Consultation in all things means that progression can be assessed from both sides and to the mutual advantage to all!

There we feel that you have had quite enough to think upon with this nights discourse. Think over what has been given to you, mull it over in your mind, discuss it if you like with other like minded brethren and see if it opens up new avenues of thought for you. Your next round of life experiences await you, prepare yourself for this journey, not into the unknown but to a familiar place of dwelling in fact, you can say coming home to your family of like souls who await your coming with joy in their hearts!!

Farewell dear Brother scribe may you receive the Blessings from the One on High. Farewell.

Chapter 13

RELIGION FOR MAN NOT GOD

August 3rd 2002 2.00 a.m.

You have been thinking we know about the life that awaits you and in fact all of mankind for that is a truth that cannot be denied. Once you are born into this life upon earth, there is only one exit and that is one that we all take in due course. It is inevitable if we are to progress as it has been intended. You feel that the more that you can understand about your coming journey the better it is, for you can then adjust yourself forewarned is forearmed, and that means that your transition can be one of joyful reunion, and you understand just what we mean we know!

Reunion not of the physical body but that of the Spirit or shall we put it, the Mind substance that goes on it's permanent journey through all of lifetimes that await you!

One day and it may come sooner that mankind realizes, he will be able to see his new life before it actually happens in reality!! With not only his inner perception but also in his earthly form!!! No, dear friend he will not actually go there and come back, but the understanding will be there of just what it is that he will eventually go to! So he will be more conscious of what it is that awaits him in the next dimension! Your schools will teach your young more of the unseen Spiritual matters that have been neglected for so long and here we do mean the so called Religious teaching! For that word has resulted in much misunderstanding on all sides! Religion if you wish to continue to call that part of man's consciousness, should encompass all forms of Religious thought. And that means a complete overhaul, a rethinking of what is fact and what is not!! For so much of Man's religious perception is flawed, he has lost what he once had, and that is his awareness of what God stands for!!! He has lost that feeling of awe and wonderment of what life is all about. He is beset with materialism on all sides, have this, get that, regardless of what it may cost him in his true peace of mind. Here we do not speak of trivial personal possessions, which at times are a necessary prop to sustain a decent lifestyle. We talk of the inner Man, the one who really knows himself as more than the empty shell that struts about the earth seeking he knows not what, but he is never completely satisfied for he feels and knows that there is a vacuum that needs to be filled with Spiritual values. Turn back to what you know is the real reality of existence and that is that this sojourn upon the lower plane of earth is but a transient one, and one that is only a stepping stone to life's true Reality which is the one that awaits him when he returns to it. For believe us, Man comes from the real world, and must eventually return to it, better equipped than when he left it. With inner knowledge and understanding. That is dear friends if he has truly understood why it is that he has incarnated upon this plane of what he feels is of woe!! When it could and should be one of joy and upliftment. Not this vain struggle to push oneself for ever up the ladder of material advancement. For in truth the really advanced individual is the one who tries to understand what it is that God is telling him via his inner consciousness and that is, that we are all ONE, in his sight. Different in race and colour yes, but within we are one not only with Him but with each other, and until Man looks upon his fellow Man as his other self and not just a stranger he will never live in complete harmony in this world of yours. There is so much that Man can achieve if he only puts his mind to it. And we are not speaking of territorial gains!! The earth is for all peoples and not just for the benefit of the rich and famous!! Within your earth lie vast treasures of natural wealth and we do not speak of what Man considers natural wealth Gold, jewels and such like, they are just baubles, playthings of a backward looking tribe. We speak of the hidden treasures of minerals, water and the life giving energy that lies beneath the surface. Tap into these natural treasures and you will find complete satisfaction for your stay upon this planet!! We can see what lies beneath your feet, but Man so far has only touched the surface as it were. Seek what is there waiting for him to use for the benefit of all. Nature is there to be used and not abused as she is at present. Learn to harness the forces, that are unleashed upon you, store up in the years of abundance for when the lean years greet you, and then you will be prepared to live in peace and harmony. You think Nature is harsh, she is not she is Natural and think about that! Learn to live with her and do not be frightened by what at present you do not understand. Man has a brain, let him use it for Man's own environment, and that means all of Mankind's. Live in harmony and then you will be able to look further at the Heavens that await you, this planet of yours could become one of them, it has the potential, make it a reality for those who are to come after you!!

We will cease here for NOW!! We bid you and your little scribe farewell again on these pages of life.

Chapter 14

THE LIFE AHEAD

August 14th 2002 2.00 p.m.

We often think as we go through life about death and what awaits us when we go through its portals! Most religions have a very hazy and somewhat escapist idea of what this life continuation is all about. And believe us when we tell you that it is a continuation and not a separation as you may imagine! You sleep as it were on one plane of existence and awake upon another. It really is as easy as that. The so called death of the body is a necessary act for the real one of you to be released and ready to continue the interrupted journey!

You will want to know what actually happens to you or rather the spirit you when you leave behind this mortal body. Well you do not suddenly become as it were a being of light able to do almost anything that you desire! There are procedures to go through! Surprises you no doubt, but this next world that you find yourself upon has rules and regulations just like the one you have just left. But here you fully understand the reasoning behind these rules etc, for they are for the benefit of the whole!!! Here you will learn that self is not the one who comes first!! Quite a shock for some of the newly arrived we can assure you!! You are gradually shown how self can be modified without it doing any harm to the one who is the self!! We now go back to the time of departure from this your earth plane, you have slept and awakened! And what is it that you "see"! Well in most cases it's a form of light that not only envelopes you but somehow brings you great comfort and a feeling of absolute security! You just surrender yourself to this wonderful essence of God's Love. You are then transported as it were to a place of rest and tranquillity. You are now in a state of non-being!! You just "are" and that is the beginning of your adjusting to your new surroundings. Time is Nothing here, so what seems like a second or two could easily be a day or more in your time scale! So forget time as time and just loose yourself in the NOW!! For that is what it is!!

We take you now to when you are fully awake to where you are! All very familiar, you recognize things that have long been forgotten but which hold dear memories for you. You now are ready to embrace as it were your dear ones of yesteryear, who have been hovering around you since you "came over" to their side of life! You have a lot of "catching up" to do, renewing old acquaintanceships and also making some new ones!! More of that later!!

Once you have gone through all those memories, you are then taken to your new abode which is your temporary home, until such times as you wish to occupy your own permanent one!! Some of your loved ones will remain with you for the time being. Others will be back to their normal routines of their life styles! For you must remember they too have their own lives to live and that includes what they may be learning or actually doing! You see life here is so very similar to your old one isn't it? With the exception you do not need to work for a living!!! You have a "job" if and when you decide that you are ready and when you have been assessed as to your capabilities!! We all have an aptitude for something, its just finding out what it is and then adjusting to what you feel that you can do!!

But before all of that can come about you are required to reassess and revaluate your recent life upon the earth plane! You have been told elsewhere about how this comes about but we will go over it again!

You are shown as it were like a living picture graph of your life's events, those that are relevant not only to yourself but how they have affected others!! You view yourself in this form of motion picture which is also in a form of three dimension. It can be stopped as it were frame by frame if you wish to study it more clearly! You are not only you in the picture but you also experience what the effect was that you had upon others, be it good or otherwise!! You then acknowledge what it is that you must do to rectify an unpleasantness or what another person did to you!! This does not involve actually "doing something" for you will find a really heartfelt feeling of sorrow is all that is needed to heal a wound by all concerned!!! "Sorry" when said with real sincerity and meaning cancels out all those past unhappy memories!! That is only a brief resume of what happens to you but out of it you become a not only better person but one who can look forward to a life of complete understanding and service to others! And service is a lovely word when viewed in 'its' right perspective!!

Do you feel that now you are ready to embark upon this new life of yours? All the old worries and tribulations are behind you what awaits you is a wonderful new life of fresh experiences and learning. You are now ready to resume your old acquaintanceships if that is what is going to help; you, also the new ones that we spoke of earlier. For here you are with your own kind" and all that that implies, you help and are being helped, everything for the present is at a leisurely pace until you are well adjusted. This requires schooling!! Don't be alarmed, you are all of the same disposition, no exams, or trying to be better than the next person, if one requires a "helping hand! Then others are only too willing to extend one. You are to be taught about the ability to Think in a positive manner! And that believe us dear friends require a lot of Thought. For upon this plane all things start with Thought. How you look how you dress how you "eat"! Oh yes, you do "eat" when and if you wish! But that is another subject. Everything and we do mean everything is not only "made up" of thought but is also "conveyed" by thought.

Our buildings, our cities, our form of transport is all from the Thought process!! So you see you have a great deal to learn if you wish to become proficient in that mode of creativity!! And also to be able to "do it" on your own without our supervision!!! Much for you to think about is there not? You were told in the beginning about your "temporary abode", well it will soon be "time" for you to take up your permanent residence!! This will all depend on where you are to be placed for your period of learning and shall we say "service". Everyone is different, some will have partners who have prepared a place for you others will perhaps want to "go it" alone for the time being. Though we must say, only a very few people wish to embark upon that lifestyle! Companionship brings out the best in all people, as you no doubt realize we hope!!

Now you think to yourself what happens to me on a day to day basis, and am I continually being monitored, do I have any time to myself and what is my leisure time made up of? All questions that require an answer, but not all "regions" of the next realm of existence live as each other!! We are not Robots, we are human beings with likes and dislikes like everyone else. You make of your life what you wish. Nothing is forced upon you but you do realize that what you do affects others and so you try to live in Harmony, for it has been proved that that is the best and only way to live a productive life!!

We think we have given you a brief understanding of what life awaits you, of course there is much much more, but like the old saying you must learn to walk before you run!!

Farewell dear friends upon the earth plane. One day you will be with us and then you will know first hand if what we have told you is anything like the Truth we know and then you too will!!

Farewell, Farewell dear little Brother, Farewell.

Chapter 15

THE LITTLE CRAFT

August 17th 2002 12.45 a.m.

We welcome you dear Brother you responded to our call and we are grateful so we will begin this night discourse with you.

Where to begin? We so often talk with you about the life to come that we feel you must think is there nothing else? Well you are right! There is nothing else! For life is forever! And we do mean forever! It never ceases! Even when you cast aside your careworn body, your real life just goes on as if nothing untoward has happened, which is true for nothing untoward has happened, you've just exchanged one garment for another that is more suitable to your new surroundings, one that can be worn and altered as when and if it is needed!! You see here upon our side of life's journey you now experience the ability to "roam" as it were in the halls of infinity!! You now begin to live as you have never lived before! No physical handicaps to hold you back from this new adventurous stage that you have embarked upon! Think of yourself as a small boat on a vast ocean, you go where the wind takes you!! But remember you are at this helm and so you are the guiding force that navigates the craft along the various shore lines of the new world, countries that you can visit!! Does that not appeal to your sense of adventure? We hope it does, for here you are travelling upon uncharted waters and where will they take you?

Do you have a map to guide you or are you going to be blown hither and thither without a compass to guide you?

We dear friend are your "compass" and we it is who will be your guides and companions upon this stage of your journey for we have charted the sea's upon which you the little craft are floating!! All very fanciful you may think but then this new life of yours is one of knowledge and yes adventure, for you do not know what is awaiting you upon this journey do you? What have the books told you about this new life of yours? Precious little we believe for it seems that man's mind has long been clouded with thoughts of what he imagines his Heaven is like, and the pictures that have been painted in the books of so called wisdom have not always been accurate! And why do you think that is? It is because no one really knows or because they have been told to withhold this information? Perhaps a little of both we feel! For you see whatever is told to you is only from a second hand viewpoint is it not? You have not yet been able to experience it at first hand, and everyone who expresses a viewpoint does so from their experience and no other!! So what are you to believe? You must sift through the information that you receive, and try to collate it into what is a simple form of logical realities! In other words, don't accept all things told you either in book form or from those who have experienced a brief sojourn in our world of existence. Piece together all the information gleaned, see if it tallies with other scraps that you have stored up and somewhere in between you will have come across a truth, and then you can start to chart your new life style that lies ahead of you!! Do not fear for we all travel along this path of knowledge and eventually we will reach that haven of rest that we all seek! You have navigated the worst part of your journey and are now in tranquil waters ready to travel further upon life's journey!! You will think to yourself just what have I been told? Has it got me any where? Well dear friend Has it? At least you should be in a better frame of mind than when we started! Though we think that what you want to hear is just how this new life of yours affects you the one who is going to live it!!!

Well we have told you that we are the one's who will navigate your craft (which is you!) along the waters that await you. You may experience tranquil seas, or you may encompass some that are shall we say somewhat turbulent, but your craft is sturdy and will come to no harm believe us. For your new life is to be one of not only learning and trying to understand, but also one of enjoyment. You are in for quite a few surprises for the life ahead of you has twists and turns, and they are all for a reason, to stimulate you into becoming wiser in all the various aspects of what this new life holds for you!!

You will unfold as it were into the person that you really are, the one that has been somewhat held back all those years upon earth!! And yet that time has not been wasted, for have you not learned the lesson of life upon that planet? And has it not given you a better understanding? Perhaps not!! You will only find out when you review that past existence won't you? We hope that it has shown you something that you can build upon in your new surroundings. Look forward to your new continuation of your previous existence, see if some of the lessons that you have learnt can be applied to your present life style? You should be able to say yes I do know how I should react to such and such a situation, for believe us dear friends situations occur here just as they have in your previous life style! You do not know exactly what awaits you, that way you grow and in growing you learn how to live life more fully!! The life upon this new realm of existence is one of joy and fulfilment, you are now in a position to alter your life style to suit not only yourself but those around you!

You begin to wonder just what is this new life style of yours going to be like? Well it has not all been planned out if that is what you imagine!! There are signpost's along the way that tell you how you are progressing, and it's entirely up to you how you chose to accept them! For it is your life and no one else's! So use it wisely so that it can benefit not only yourself but all of the others that you come into contact with!! You see dear friend life has continued has it not? You are still in command of it, only here you are able to see ahead just a little bit more and so you will see a mistake before it is made and so you can avoid it instead of being put off by it!! You probably think "Oh dear, it all sounds so familiar to my old life style and I thought Heaven was going to be such a nice place!!!" Well dear friend, if this is what you call Heaven, then it is a nice place, but it is one where you are not idle! And, let us face it, you would not want to be would you? Your aim is to progress! And to do that you have to be active, so think to yourself that being alive is being active and not passive! You have so much to look forward to once you have become used to the new surroundings. You start out on a given journey one that you if you did but know, you have mapped out by your own previous life upon earth! Think upon that dear friend, your journey began there on its upward journey back to where it all started. And the realm that you now find yourself upon is just one of many that you will travel to in your journey back home. Is not this life wonderful in its gradual continuation in its ever upward spiral? We feel that it is time to bid you farewell on this part of your journey and we will resume it in the future, so for the present we bid you all Farewell and may God's blessings be upon one and all Farewell, Farewell, Farewell.

Chapter 16

LIFE CONTINUES

August 18th 2002 Morning

We bid you welcome dear Brother. You have been thinking to yourself what is it that I can tell to others to give them a better understanding of what awaits them on the other side of this earthly life. Well dear friend you are doing your best, with our assistance, but remember not all people are yet ready to understand the full reality of the life that awaits them when at last they depart this earthly one. They have read and so therefore tend to think that what they have read and been told is "Gospel!!!"

When in reality it is only a form of supposition on the part of the illustrator of what he or she has either partly experienced or shall we say thought of as likely to be what they hope it is!!!

Not everything to do with our world (which is also yours!) is shall we say cut and dried. Life progress's all the time, and what was applicable in the forgotten past it not relevant to today's standards! You see dear friend, we too move on we do not stand still, either in thought or action!! For how else are we to progress unless we keep pace with the times! Much for you to think upon! What suited Man two thousand years ago, I am afraid does not always apply to his thinking and acting in today's life style, and yet there is much that is still relevant and if put into today's vernacular will be accepted by today's thinking man, even if he imagines that what he is thinking is entirely New! Nothing is, it is just that it is viewed in a different perspective! What you term as progress! But progress does not mean throwing away the baby with the bathwater!!! You understand our meaning we know!! You in the West have some very apt sayings that we too understand and use!! Though at times we find some of them slightly amusing and not always accurate!!!

Many people have an idea that somehow Heaven and they still tend to call this next phase of their development that, is somewhat still like the medieval paintings and those stained glass windows that all seem to convey Heaven as being peopled by either Heavily winged Angles or people in long flowing garments and somewhat so called Angelic expressions on their faces! We are not like that! At least those of today who have "passed over". We are of today that it our thinking we do not dwell in the past, if we did, we would not be relevant to today's thinking would we? We too have to move with the times, even if some of us would like to remain in the past, where everything seemed rosy, but did it really? We like to think of it as so, but all periods in ones life has its good and bad times, for that is part of life and growing up!!!

Yes dear friend we still have a lot of growing up to do even here incidentally elsewhere also!! Nothing ever stands still, it is forever changing and being re-evaluated, so what was past is now part of the now, it has not been lost, first re-assessed and shall we say updated!!

One tends to think that when you transfer to our plane everything is ordered and in place as it were that is old, trusted and tried, then one will feel secure, but that is only until you have become accustomed to your new life. Then you can see that it is not quite as you imagined. It is full of surprises, and challenges, and you are now in the throes of an exiting new life style, that will not only test your imagination but also will help you to grow not only in thought but also in deed!!

Life must go on and not remain inactive. Accept that this new round of experiences is for your own good. You are gradually broadening your horizons if fact you are maturing in every sense of the word! So you see dear friend the life ahead of you is still worth living and striving for, is it not? Do not go on thinking rosy thoughts of what you imagine Heaven is like for this is NOT! That heaven! There are the so called Heavens but this first one that you find yourself upon when leaving the physical body is Not heaven, though to some it may appear like one! They will learn and then they will know that the life started upon earth goes on, yes even here but oh so different and yet in some ways very like the one you have just left!! So accept that your life here continues, better than the one you have left, but still one of challenges, and overcoming shall we say difficulties though they are never insurmountable, just tests to keep you active and alive! There's such a lot for you to learn, and enjoy in the learning. No, not all learning, so do not think that you have a lifetime ahead of you of continual learning what it is all about!! There is more freedom here than you ever experienced upon earth. Enjoy your new round of life upon our world, for there is much to see and marvel at. Things that are beyond your widest imaginings and dreams. So much for you to enjoy and yes learn from!! For even when you are enjoying yourself you are still learning are you not? New lifestyles that will amaze you, places and people to visit and not all of the same culture, does that surprise you? As we have said life goes on. But all is harmonious never forget that. You belong here as do all of those other people, learn to live in that way and you will find that perhaps you are in a form of Heaven after all!!! We bid you Brethren of the earth Farewell.

We feel we will leave you on that note, it has been a pleasure for us to be with you little Brother, farewell and remember You are never really alone one of us is always near, Farewell dear friend Farewell.

Chapter 17

OTHER SPHERES

August 19th 2002 1.40 a.m.

Take up your pen my friend, for we are here and are ready for you. Welcome little Brother welcome to another nights discourse.

Think, what is it that you wish us to talk to you about? Yes we know that you have been thinking over in your mind these last few days about the sort of life that awaits all peoples when they leave the earth plane and travel to what you know as the Spirit World! Yes you are right, each World or Earth if you wish to call it that, has what is known as its Spiritual counterpart! They do not impinge upon another so called Spirit world for each world is progressing in its own way and so though they are in their "Spirit World" it is not the same as "yours" or rather the one that belongs to your earth! This is not to be confused with other "planets" that orbit around the various Suns in your Universe! Planets are Earths in various disguises and are Not spirit places of existence! They are inhabited by physical entities and it is only when their life span upon that particular planet has ended that they then transfer like yourselves to their Spiritual counterpart, and so the spiral is set in motion for them! Now you wonder, do you, as Spirit entities go to these planet's? Well yes and no, for if you are to visit them then you go as Spirit and not as a physical vehicle! But if it has been decided to enhance your progress then you are materialized upon that Planet as a physical soul and not as a Spirit one!! For as a Spirit visitor you would NOT be observed by the inhabitants, or rather only by those with the inner sight. But as a permanent resident upon that Plane of existence you would be a solid body of observation! Like those other inhabitants! ! Do you follow what we are saying to you?

"Spirit" and we still call you by that name is not the same as the physical vehicle! Confusing for you no doubt. But as Spirit you dwell within the perimeter of the Spirit Worlds and not the Planets that you are told exit in outer space!!!

Difficult for us to convey to you exactly what we mean. Imagine a piece of fruit that has a skin to it, you start to peel that skin and it ends up as a twirling piece that is separate from the body of the fruit. It is part of it but is now different for it has been separated, but it still belongs. Well, the Spirit skin as it were is that part of you that has been separated from the main body of the physical person!! You are now that piece of floating twisting skin like person. While the body remains intact!! And is now separate from what is the real you!! You are the skin and not now the body. Though that body can be resumed as an entity if it should be required! But would now be modified!! That is if you are to take up residence upon another sphere and need a permanent solid body of identity!!! Spirit remains a spirit and must not be confused with another "physical vehicle"!!! As spirit you now remain as such!! Going from one Spirit sphere to another which is in your orbit and not another's!! You remain in your spiral for that is where you are progressing. Others as we have said have their spirals and unless it has been deemed necessary for your progression to become part of their life style you will not inhabit it!! As a physical vehicle.

As we have said, you may visit these other spheres but NOT in "physical" form, only as an observer! Do you follow what we are saying? The physical and we still call a body of lower density physical is separate from the Spirit even though the Spirit inhabits a physical body when necessary! Your other Planets are inhabited by being's like yourselves but of a higher degree but still as it were physical and subject to those laws of existence! If you as human entities eventually contact those others or even vice versa, you will do so as physical beings and not as Spirit entities!!! Though should you remain permanently upon those spheres you will become subject to their laws and vibrations and so become part of their spiral of existence separate from your original earth one!!!

Sounds complicated to you no doubt, but that is all part of the Universal law of existence!! Much for you to try and understand! We know of these other spheres, and yes we visit them but only as Spirit Entities for we are part of your worlds spiral and we do not wish to become part of another's! Only in as much as it is of interest to us to see how they progress and if we can learn anything from them!! That is from the "Spiritual stand point". You see dear friend's upon the earth these is much for you to discover about not only yourselves but others as well!! This is all a vast vast enterprise and one that cannot be fully understood until you progress from the lower spheres of density to those of Higher vibration and understanding!! Life is simple and yet complicated it is not? There are as we have said "Universal laws" and we must all learn to live within them, its not at all difficult when you learn to understand this underlying principle of existence and what it is all about!! You wonder if we can co exist with these other brethren upon those other dimensions? Yes, we can if we and they choose too. All part of the experience of living but one has to have "grown up" as it were not only physically but mentally before one can embark upon that life style!! Be content with what you will have and then you will be able to understand more and decide what it is you wish to do, and more importantly what is deemed right for you to do, if you wish to progress in a certain direction!!!!

What a lot for you to understand once you have been liberated from your earthly body is there not? But just think of the excitement of it all. You really will begin to live when you have left that gross body behind won't you? We feel that we will end this discourse there for you have much to think about and wonder about and see if you can make sense of all that has been imparted to you this night!

We bid you farewell!!! Little scribe, do not think about all this until you wake on the morrow or rather later today on your world!!! Farewell dear friend and Brother Farewell.

Chapter 18

Home

August 22nd 2002 2.00 a.m.

I am ready if you wish to contact me!
Yes dear Brother we do!
Welcome to this nights discourse!!

What is it that awaits you when it is your time to depart from this plane called Earth? You wonder because there are so many variations on the same theme that you feel bewildered and wonder what is real and what is not. The reality is that you have left the body that you call physical and are ready to clothe yourself in your new one that you call Spirit!! What a wonderous thing that is! For now you can really begin to live and not just exist!!

You leave the old and the new is already you, bathed in clouds of soft and warm vapour that swirl around you, comforting you and taking you along with them, you no longer think where am I? What is happening to me? You accept you are in a form of "Non Being" neither one thing nor the other. The clouds envelope your whole being, you are light in fact you *are* the light, you search for your body and realize that you just *are*. You no longer need your old gross vehicle that has served you all these years, you are now free from its toils, you are You, you are wafted along as it were through clouds of misty hues all colours soft and hazy and warm, you just want to drift and that is exactly what you are doing. Through light and vapour that is somehow solid and yet is not, you hear voices and yet you see no one, yet you do not feel alone. There seem to be arms, soft and gentle easing you along this pathway to your new abode. Will you ever get there? You do not really care for you are at peace at last and the thought of yesterday are the realities of tomorrow! Today is yours and you are content!

Time to awake!! You cease your travelling, you are now upright and looking around you. Are there people? You recognise voices but as yet you cannot put faces to them, for they come and go as in a dream! You feel a soft and gentle hand upon your shoulder, you turn and see for the first time the figure of one who is nameless and yet you feel you have known them forever. The figure beckons you to follow and so you seem to drift not with the figure but part of it, for it is the You that has awaited your coming. You *are here* at last! All around you is a soft light that continually changes, from soft iridescent hue's, to deep and beautiful gold, that not only is, but sounds like distant harps, the light is alive as it were, and the sounds bathe you in their music, you are now part of what is!! Faces appear to you, loved ones of long ago there is a sound of soft laughter as if to say Welcome, welcome, welcome home, safe at last!

All around now are sounds that are familiar and yet you cannot remember where you heard them last. You are still moving along what seems to be a pathway of soft velvet that feels so comforting, you look at your feet for you have sunk deeply into this form of soft like earth but your feet seem like the vapour of the clouds that wafted you along!! No matter for those around you are just as you are, you are being propelled towards a building that seems to shimmer in the glow of a sunset, the building not large but very beautiful, not one colour but all colours that take on different shades, from palest gold, to deep deep sapphire blue, and then to a soft emerald green, and then back to gold. The gardens in front of the building are a green that you have never seen before and it is alive and sounds like falling water, you are gently ushered into the coolness of the building which to you seems like a temple of some sort. Inside there is a large courtyard with a fountain that seems to be suspended in the air for it has no beginning and no end, just gentle sprays of different colours and sounds, you are then escorted by friends and loved ones to an inner room, there are cushions but no furniture, just lovely soft cushions all around, music seems to be in the air, you sit or recline amongst the billowing softness of the cushions, you are now alone, except for a light that seems to glow and move back and forth and as you watch you see that it envelopes a figure whose face is just beginning to be seen, a face of pure love. The smile is one of serenity and the eyes are blue and soft and gentle and here you feel at peace. The light comes nearer and nearer until you are part of it and yet not, and you feel rather than be told that you are here to rest, you look for the figure, no it has not gone but you cannot see it for you are now part of it! Slumber becon's you, you drift into a gentle sleep, and you know that when you awake you are now Alive as you have never been before and ready and refreshed to start the new long journey back to the source of All Creation. You are here, this is your new home. Welcome dear one Welcome we have waited a long time for you, let us now begin this new life together!!

Chapter 19

Mortal and Immortal

August 26th 2002 12.35 a.m.

Welcome dear Brother in Christ. We bid you welcome and may the blessings of the One on High be upon you and within you now and forever.

The one you call Jesus of Nazareth the one who was so cruelly put to death but who was revived upon the third day to live as it were forever in the minds of Mankind. A symbol of God's love for his creations. You never really die, for it is just this shell that is left behind to disintegrate and return to the dust from which it came. The spirit the true self can never die for it is indestructible, it is the very body of the Creator of all things! And as that part it can never, never, be destroyed.

Altered, yes and that is as it should be for this journey that began upon the Earth plane must finish there before it can be released to continue 'its' journey in the world of what you choose to call Spirit!

So much conjecture is generated with that one word "Spirit" and yet it need not be looked upon as something strange and unreal. For in truth Spirit is more of a reality than ever the mortal body was! For "Spirit" is that very essence of the One on High that we spoke of. The real life force that is never quenched! The body that is the so called physical one is the one that has to be used while the Spirit is in it's temporary home upon the Earth. One day and that will not be for a very long time the Spirit as it is called will be the only body needed here upon your plane of Earth. For Man will have learnt the lesson that he is made of the Divine Essence and no longer needs the gross body that has been his habitation in the past. For the Earth will have ceased to be looked upon as a gross and dense planet for it will then be one of lighter substance and vibration!

You see dear friends, not only will Man have advanced in that respect but his home upon Earth will also have altered to keep pace with his evolution! The Earth is not a static place of habitation it *lives* the same as you do, it grows, it alters it becomes more "Spiritual" if that is the right word! Like your Universe it is *never* still! There is far more going on than you can ever realize!

The Universe and that means not just the atmosphere that you term space, wherein dwell all the planets and their subordinate structures for believe us a *planet* is not just a *planet* it has its counterpart that keeps it going!!! All the time there is energy being pumped into it to keep it not only in orbit but to help it to live!! Your body is like a small reflection of your Universe! It has to have energy to keep it in orbit upon the planet Earth! You are a micromism of the macrocosm and that is but a small part of the Whole!!!

Mankind tries to fathom out what these galaxies and other planets are and how they may be invaded by Him, instead of looking within himself and seeing the world that he wishes to conquer is in reality his very self!!! Once Mankind learns the lesson of who and what he is in relation to those around him then and only then will he be in a position to explore what he thinks is His Universe, which it is not *His* to explore!! He may travel to other places or planets of interest but he must first make sure that they can sustain His form of life!! Would you really wish to spend the rest of your existence in some form of vast bowl like structure and not be able to venture out of it without some form of heavy garment surrounded by wires and such like!! He must search for a place that he can live upon in freedom otherwise he may just as well be content with what he has got!! Cease these probes into the far far distance for they will avail him naught! Man must put his own house in order first and when we say "his own house" we refer to himself as well as the planet!!!

There is so much that Man can do to make the life upon this Earth of yours a fit dwelling place for *All of Mankind* before he can cast his eyes with envy upon unknown places of existence where if he did but know it he would not only be not welcome, but on which he could not even exist unless encased in some metal like garment! Believe us not all planets are inhabited by "beings" that can be seen with the physical eyes of man!! Think upon that dear friends! You can be seen but can *you see*? There is much to be learnt before you will be allowed this yearning for exploration to be realized!! Go back to the beginning of this discourse! Man must be of a spiritual nature in fact he must eventually shed this Mortal body and live upon your Earth as a Spirit Entity before he can venture further into the unknown!!

Your fictional picture books of what is thought to be not only beings but actual places of existence have no relation to *what* and *who* is actually *OUT THERE*. We say again to you Put your own house in order first and then you can think about this PASSION for exploration!! Man is still in his infancy in spite of what he may think. There have been others before him and where are they now?!! They too thought that they were ready to explore but where did it get them? Lost civilizations!! See to it that yours does not become one of them!!

We began with Jesus of Nazareth who showed that the *body* is not the only one that Man possesses but that it is the Spirit within that is the real Man. Think upon that, one day you too can become that living Spirit in reality and can cast aside THE Mortal Body forever!!

Live for one another, care for one another, you are all from the same Divine Source, treat each other with love and compassion become what you know you can be, but it is *you* that has to do the trying you cannot leave it all to others!!

We bid you farewell dear earth friends, we bid you all farewell. Peace be with you!! And with you little scribe and with you. Farewell.

Chapter 20

LIFE CONTINUES

August 29th 2002 2.40 a.m.

We welcome you dear Brother we welcome you. Tonight we wish to talk to you about the life upon not only your Earth plane and the one above it that you call the Spirit World but also those others that are as yet unknown to you. When you start your journey back to its source you begin with the Earth plane, this to many people is all that there is to life. Live while you can and do not trouble yourself what may or may not come after it!! But to those who think deeply about the reason for them being upon the Earth plane of existence they not only believe in the next one but they want to know more about it, for it is their next dwelling place and that well may be for some considerable time in your earth time scale!! Though in reality time is of no special importance once you have transferred yourself to this new life!! But what sort of life is it that beckons you? Is it anything like the one upon Earth? Or is it like a fairyland where nothing is impossible to those who believe!!! Afraid not dear friend for here life is made up of the same rules and regulations and yes even laws, that you had upon Earth! For if there were not THESE safeguards you would soon find that chaos would rule!! No dear friend everything is ordered and well thought out for your own benefit! You are here to learn and to progress in your upward spiral of Evolution and that means not only study but work!! Yes work!!

Not the manual variety but of the mind!! Your "work" shall we say begins once you have become adjusted to your new life style, which quite honestly is not so very different from you old one!! You come into contact with all sorts of people, and not all of them do you feel you wish to make friends of! Others, you immediately have a "rapport" with, you gradually learn which ones to associate with and which to avoid. Now this is not to say that those with whom you do not seem to wish to know are in any way bad they are just "not your sort" the same as you are not theirs!!!

So you see there is plenty of adjusting to be achieved on *all* sides!! As you have been told before in other discourses, you gravitate to the like minded and so that is how you will progress. You learn to "learn" from them because of their EXPERIENCE of this life upon the next world! They have much to offer you, as you in your turn will have to give to them!! You are accepted as you are and that is when you begin to live this new life!

We have said "learning" but that does not imply the sort of learning that is taught in schools! Your learning comes from living and learning to live and let live. But all the time you are accumulating knowledge that will enhance your life style and carry you forward to your next domain!

Your previous life upon the Earth plane prepared you for this one had you but realized it! Just by "living" is an art in itself. It is learning how to "get on" with others and adapt to the situation's that confront you in life! The same applies here! You have situations that come upon you quite unaware, and you have to deal with them. So you see life is much the same as before, except that here you will know how to deal with any unknown situation almost before it arrives!! Your "intuition" has been heightened, you not only view but are part of any given form of situation, so you can adapt to it with comparative ease!!

Now do not imagine that situations as it were are continually cropping up all the time, they just occur as a matter of course and are not put there as a test or hurdle for you to overcome! They are just normal and natural occurrences! And must be accepted as such! So you see dear friends your "days" if you like to call these spaces of time are fairly ordinary aren't they? Just routine as it were! You are now living as you have always done, but you are more aware of what that means here you learn how to *control* your life and make it work for you. You are *not* at the mercy of the unexpected! For as we have said you are aware of it before it has happened! So you are learning aren't you? There is a great deal more to life "over here" than you can ever visualize in your wildest dreams, but it is all "ordered" make no mistake about that, but it does *not* seem like it in any way whatsoever! Everyone learns very quickly to *adapt* for it is the right and proper way to live here. You "work" (though that is not the right word) at what suits you best, you are shown various options and do not think that you are restricted to one form only, if it does not suit you then you are free to change it, it is all for the benefit of your Spiritual growth which is the main reason that you are even here! We are your teachers and friends, though you are not usually aware that that is our capacity for work. Teaching others by example is what we do we do *not* stand in front of a blackboard with a stick pointing out various things!! Just by example that is our method and we find it works very well, for many of our "pupils" opt to become teachers in their own right!! There is so much for you to see and do and become a part of that your "days" just fly past!! *Nothing bores* you over here you do not have to *fill in time* for there never seems enough of it to some people!!

This life is still only a preparation for the *ones* to come but you will have learnt very valuable lessons that will enable you to adapt very easily to that next round of lifestyles, where more will be expected of you because of what you have been learning. So you see each *life cycle* is really a continuation of the previous one, it never really ends, it just *alters* until the final stage when you *know who* and *what you are* and *why* you are! But that dear friends is a very very long way off in your Earth time scale!!! And this is where we bid you farewell for this nights discourse!! We trust that we have given you something to think about, and yes work upon while you tarry upon the sphere of Earth. Farewell dear friends and Farewell to the little scribe Farewell and may Gods blessing be with you. Farewell.

Chapter 21

RELIGIOUS UNDERSTANDING

September 2nd 2002 Afternoon

We left you the other day promising that we would continue with our discourse on your life to come. That does not just mean yours we are talking in general terms. We left you where you are to begin your new life's training. This will involve quite a lot of hard thinking on your part! Nothing of any value comes easily, it has always required an effort on the part of the person who is seeking the deeper mysteries of Life! As on Earth, so it is here. Only here you are now in possession of shall we say "powers" though that does not express the true nature of these learned attributes. Powers to many people conjure up thoughts of magic and the suchlike! Here there is no magic. It is understanding the fundamental laws of all of existence!

Once you begin to understand them and yes live by them, then you truly will be in possession of those so called "powers". We told you of "projects" that are in progress that you may find suit your particular aptitude. There are *always* ongoing projects, that not only broaden your mind but help you to understand one of the reasons for your being here in the first place! As we told you, you are free to choose what you feel suits you, and you are not confined to just one project, vary them if you wish. In fact some "pupils" for that is what you will be though perhaps we should have said "co-workers" and "partners", come up with fresh ideas that are put before those who deal with these subjects, and if considered viable and worthwhile then they are adopted!

So you see dear friends there is plenty of scope for those who have a talent that needs to be exploited for the "common good"! Remember that, everything is for that purpose is it not? You begin to wonder what these so called "projects" are all about. They represent thoughts that are being put into practice not only for those upon the realms of Spirit, but also upon those others your Earth one included!! Much can be achieved from "our side" so that it can be put into practice where it is most needed, and where it will do the most good.

Projects are always ongoing they do not stand still once the objective has been reached, for often that supports another one and so it goes on and on! Life as you can see is very full and is never, never, dull!

We mentioned "places" which in reality are other "countries" on our globe! You will be amazed at the contrasts that exist here, even more so than those upon Earth! You will have ample time to not only visit these other habitations but you can if you wish "enrol" as it were for work in that particular "country". Where you will find people like yourself but also different. Just as upon Earth! You don't change completely just because you take on your Spirit garment. There are people of different races, colours and cultures! And oh yes "Religions". You wonder about that for we expect you thought once on the Spirit Realm all Religions became one!! No, not yet anyway. All Religions have one thing in common they all stem from God and eventually must return to him as *ONE*. But remember *diversity* doesn't mean *animosity*. Here all forms are tolerated and understood for what they are and for what they are seeking to achieve! *Tolerance* in all things and in that way you learn to live and let live and yes *learn*. For everyone has something to contribute to our life here. You may find that some "areas" are not quite what you have expected, for shall we say some of the inhabitants of those areas are not so "advanced" as others, and they need special love and attention and believe us they do receive it.

So you see there is another worthwhile project to pursue. Remember dear friends not all of the Spirit Realm is one of light. There are dark areas where you would need special tuition if you wished to venture there and even then you would never go alone but always in the company of others and those from the *Higher Realms of Light and understanding.* These places are not shunned, but they are kept as it were at arms distance.

There are various projects that are set up for the inhabitants to help them to progress and leave the dark areas for lighter ones on their evolutionary journey of life!

Now for something in a different vein. There is an area to the West of where we are that is very beautiful and tranquil. It is the Living Museums of all the known and unknown Religions of Mankind. Here amidst surroundings of great beauty are temples and buildings, cathedrals and humble churches, where all the history of that particular religious group is shown, and where you are invited to partake of their different cultures, without any from of coercion!! Inside the various buildings there is a form of cinematography activity, only here it takes the form of three dimensional and you are part of it though not actually "taking part". You are an observer, and treated as such with courtesy and understanding. The whole area is one of such mystical and Spiritual tranquillity that just to be there is an upliftment in every sense of the word. And you will no doubt be surprised when we tell you that the overall similarity of all of these Religions impresses you greatly!!

You come back as if from a Religious retreat, refreshed and with a deeper understanding of the meaning of *God!!* There are houses of rest, for this is a pilgrimage and you cannot hope to "take it all in" at once, and here you will meet fellow travellers from all over the globe, so you can exchange ideas and make new and lasting friendships! Yes and visit each other at other times! You see dear friends life here really is wonderful is it not? There is so much to see and do and all to help you in your progress on this realm of existence that to some they wish to remain forever for to them this is the Heaven they've always dreamed of! But dear friends it is not, you may think of it as one of the many that await you on your upward spiral of evolution. We feel that we have given you a brief outline of some of the things that await you when it is your time to leave that mortal body behind and take on your new Spiritual body of real and lasting substance!

Farewell dear friends. Remember your real life awaits you, do not fear for it will be your permanent one for all time!!

Farewell little Brother scribe, farewell!

Chapter 22

TRUE AND FALSE

September 7th 2002 12.40 a.m.

We speak to you not of the Spirit World but of the one that dwells within you! For in truth dear friend though your physical body dwells in the World you call Earth, within that body there dwells another world, a world of less reality but nevertheless one that you do inhabit and that is with the mind! We have spoken to you before about this illusive organ that cannot be perceived and yet exists within us all, for it is "that" that goes on forever, it never "dies" you call it your Spirit, well if that helps you to understand what to many would pose a difficulty then continue to call the mind your Spirit. It makes no difference what "it" is called it remains the same. For "Mind" is the traveller in this Universe of discovery! Think upon that and you will realize that what is said is the truth and nothing less! When you leave the physical body behind and enter once more upon the plane of light you are no longer a physical entity but a substance of the world you know as Spirit!! You now posses that spark of the Divine that allows you to travel from sphere to sphere, in the ever upward spiral of knowledge and understanding. Though we tell you that those two attributes do not come to you lightly. You have to work for them and with what you ask? Why with your mind substance that governs your new body of Spirit light and essence!! So you see that illusive little being called Mind is ever present, no matter what garb you choose to put on, be it Spirit or be it physical. That is your governing force. For it is the mind that generates all of the "thought power" that enables you to function on this plane of illusion and understanding!! A paradox you may think for if this sphere is one of illusion how can it also be one of understanding? Think about that little friend illusion has to be understood before you can overcome it and face the reality of where you now exist. This plane that you now inhabit has many many facets to it, and not all of them are what you might call reality! And yet even an illusion has somewhat an aspect of reality otherwise you would not be able to understand why it is called illusion!! Do not be confused with that word for it does not represent what you upon Earth call illusion, there it is done to deceive the eye, here it is in a form that the inner eye of perception is used to differentiate what is real and what might seem to be real but is not! This is all to do with the mind and how you perceive what it is that is observable to you!!! You are now in possession of not only inner sight but also the ability to piece together what it is that you perceive! And that not always with shall we say the outer sight!!

You are shown just what it is that is the real life upon this plane and what is that might be termed the imaginary one!! Yes you have written the correct word for imagination plays a very big part in life wherever it is happened to be living!! The mind is responsible for this term, for all things start with an image of what it is that you wish it to be!!! And when you have learnt the lesson of how to use that faculty and to use it properly then begins the lesson of illusion and all its potentials!! For you see dear friends here you can create illusion when you know how. You learn to "see" what is the real that is about you and what is only in your mind!!! Much for you to think about and ponder upon!!

Upon Earth the only people who create illusions for to deceive the eye are called magicians are they not? You witness what it is that they do, and you marvel at how they can deceive you right in front of your eyes!! Well upon the sphere of light, illusion can seem like a reality until you learn that it is not!! And how do you do this? By learning how to create an illusion that looks and behaves like reality!! This world to which you have come is full of wonders and you are taught by trial and error to understand what is true and what is false, and that must not be misunderstood, "true and false" are the same coin in reverse!!! We must not confuse you with riddles, for it would be so easy to do. You have to learn to be observant and know when to accept the real and to ignore the other!! It is difficult for us to give you a precise definition of what we term illusion. For has it not been said before that what to one is reality to another is illusion!! And vice – versa!!! Much to learn, but once the learning has been accomplished then the life here is one of great joy and achievement, and is always forward looking. The reason for your sojourn upon this plane is to prepare you for higher things, in other words your next round of incarnations. No, not upon the physical plane of existence but upon those higher realms that await you in your progression ever upward!! You see incarnation does not only apply to the Earth plane, for when we are living in the world of the Spirit we may be required to incarnate upon that sphere many times before we are ready to progress to those other realms that we term Higher! Where there is *No illusion*, but higher understanding of the true reality of that particular sphere. From here onwards, Reality is the only true form, there is no room for wistful illusion of any kind.

We feel that that is as far as we are permitted to take you on this nights discourse. Too much could be too confusing, so be content with what has been give to you and know that the Truth that we impart is *The Truth*, be sure of that. For one day you too will be able to verify what has been said this night!!! We bid you Farewell.

Farewell little students of the Earth, farewell, and to that one whose work it is to instruct, Farewell, may Gods blessings be upon you. Farewell.

Chapter 23

DIMENSIONS

September 9th 2002 1.40 a.m.

Dear Dear Brother in Christ, we welcome you once again. Be at peace, we are here to help you and you will not be able to intrude your own thoughts upon this nights discourse for we are in control of them, so have no fear that you will influence them. We are here to see that you do not!! We understand that you think is this all my imagination, am I really being used as they say I am. Be sure dear friend, this is NOT your imagination it is a reality, and a reality of our minds that are in control, and you are the passive instrument at the end of a long line of "instruments" that have volunteered for this kind of work!!

We begin. First we say again Welcome dear Brother, welcome, you have thought to yourself if this world that you now dwell upon is real, can the one to which you next visit upon and yes, will stay upon, can that also be as real as this present one? Believe us dear friend if you think your present one is real, you have no idea what real reality is like. For our World which is also *yours* has far more reality to it that ever the Earth world has! We really do *live* we *really* do! We are not illusions or wishful thinking of a disordered brain. *We* are living, breathing, ordinary human beings, but here we are free from the restrictive body of flesh! That limits all of your functions! You now have complete freedom of activity when you are upon this Spirit planet of pure existence!

There is no restriction of either your "body" or mind! You

notice we say "body" and that is what you still inhabit!! No not quite the physical vehicle that restricted you upon Earth, but it is its "replica" if you like, it is for you to use as a vehicle of movement and "reference". You have to be able to see and be seen as it were, you are not just a vaporous cloud of indistinct feature! This is not an ethereal planet, it is a Solid one of true reality! That no doubt makes you wonder how can it be solid and real!! Well it is dear friend, for it is not just a continuation of your present world, it is the Prototype for it!!! Yes prototype! *Ours* is the real world and yours the shadow of it!!! Yours has the denseness of your planet for that is how it has been conceived. *Ours* is the reality and yours but the *illusion* not the other way around, as is so often what is portrayed by your so called "thinkers"!!! If as one day it will be, the two Worlds will *integrate* yours to become a more spiritual form of existence and one that can be identified with "ours", for as we have told you before, the people who will inhabit your planet will be of a higher form of humanity and will be able to move as it were from one vibratory dimension to the next and back again in a normal fashion!! Death of the physical will be no more than a transition from one form of existence to another, the "body" will just resume its "natural" self and the so called physical will just fade and disappear, nothing more, it will be like the shedding of one old skin for the new one to take its place!! Where in fact it has always been, just below the surface as it were!!! Your idea of reality then will be quite, quite different. No more wondering what this next dimension is all about for you will be inhabiting both at the same time!! Do not try to fathom how that can be, for it will not come about for many, many millenniums of your Earth time!! Man has to undergo much before he can assume the dual role of Earthman and Spirit counterpart!!! It will come about for it has been programmed to do so, but as we have said it will be in the far far off distant future. Your World has to undergo much *change* it has to be purged of its denseness and allowed its Spiritual side to come to the fore!! There will be upheaval of all kinds but from out of it will emerge a cleaner finer and better dwelling place for "Spirit man" to inhabit!!

The so called Planet Earth will alter its shape!! It will become less dense, less harsh in its climatic condition, your seas will not only become cleaner, but also more *transparent* and more "liveable" yes we do say liveable! For by then man will understand how he can live under the sea as well as upon it!!! You wonder how that can be!! No, he will not sprout fins and have gills in his body! But his body will have been adapted so that he can breathe as it were in a "normal fashion" as he does now!! For the seas will have more life force within them that can be utilized by the then present population!! Do not try to think how that will come about, but it will! Man then will be capable of many things that you at present think of as only being able to be performed by those on the Spirit plane!!! When "he" has become as it were amalgamated with his Spirit form so that it is a reality as well as a form of non physical being, then he will be capable of these mysteries, for they will not then be only confined to those other worlds that you dream about!!!

There is so much that will one day transpire *but* this all takes "time" in you scale of understanding and can not be hastened, if it is to be of a permanent nature. These are future events that are in the future and not the foreseeable *Now*! But that is not to say that Mankind cannot plan for that future time! He has so much to learn, not only about himself but about the environment in which he lives! He must be able to live with Nature and yes harness her untold Energy and force, which can and will be used to revitalize your barren areas that are not only in existence now but will be even more so if you do not learn your lessons of co-operation with her. Do *not* destroy what you cannot replace in your own lifetime!! *Keep a balance* otherwise your planet will be one of lifelessness for millenniums to come!! No, man will not disappear, but many of his brother species will for their habitation will have been squandered and will not sustain their life anymore!! Think about it carefully. Do not make of your Earth a Zoo like place of existence for your animal populations! Live alongside of them they are not just living fossils to be observed through glass like structures! As things of the past!!!! That also goes for Man himself! Think about that!!

Start *Now* revitalize your Earth take care of what you put into it for it has a habit of changing its toxicity and can become not only poisonous to the Earth but also to those who dwell upon it and yes from it also!!! Cease your warlike activity, look to your planet for its life giving properties and do not destroy them for ultimately you are destroying your very selves!!!

And who will come after you?? And more to the point, Where will they have to come from to take over the mantle of Mankind!!

Enough, we are told, Enough!! You have been given ample warning see that you profit from it. We bid you Farewell and think upon that word. Fare-well and what it really means!!

Little Brother fare the well and may the blessings of the one on High be upon you.

Chapter 24

THE JOURNEY

October 1st 2002 6.35 a.m.

We welcome you Dear Brother on this fine morning!! You know doubt wonder, why this particular hour of the day? We felt that you needed a full nights rest and so we have chosen this early morning as an experiment for you!

For us, time does not really matter, but we know that it is relevant to those upon the Earth plane.

We shall now begin our talk with you, and it will be about the continuation of your lifespan upon the realms of higher knowledge and understanding! Leaving the Earth plane behind and stepping out onto the new one can be a very traumatic experience for most people. They just cannot accept that their form of life has just continued as before but in another dimension!! They do not believe that they are still very much alive and with all of their so called faculties intact!! To some it takes a very long time to adjust to this new sensation, to others they just step out as if it is perfectly normal, which it is believe us. For so much has been written regarding the so called after life and most of it is quite misleading, though perhaps not intentionally! For to most people upon Earth the idea of this "continuation" of their life form is somewhat of an anathema. They observe their body, they feel their limbs and think to themselves this is me but where am I? Am I dreaming? Where is this place? Everything strikes them as not only normal but somewhat familiar, that is all for a purpose, it is to help the newly arrived to feel at home and not to feel uneasy as to what has happened to them! It is a jolt to the personality to realize that they no longer exist upon their previous homeland called Earth. This new abode is no different in looks to them and so they have to adjust their way of thinking as to what their so called death of the body means to them!! Of course in actual fact, they are no longer a physical human being, they have transferred to the realm of so called Spirituality whatever that may mean to them!! For to the majority of people when you speak to them of the Spirit World, they have absolutely no real idea of what that term involves. For so long, they have been told that "Heaven" for that is what most people are led to believe that this next realm is, is one where everything is of a spiritual nature, where all struggles cease and everything is peaceful and almost non existant! Well dear friends, this next realm is not like that at all!! It is a working extension of your previous one, one that demands your full attention and understanding. You have much to unlearn about your new domain of existence!!

Though here we hasten to tell you, that though it is an extension it is not basically the same, for here all forms of existence vibrate at a higher level, though this does not appear so at your first encounter with those upon this realm of light!! Your new perception is gradual and you are allowed time to adjust, for after all this is now your new form of life existence, you are now *here*, in a way it is like going to a new country just like when you were upon Earth. All is strange and yet in a way familiar. The terrain looks just the same but somehow different. There is so much more light that you have no difficulty in viewing distance, it appears to you as if you are looking through a vast magnifying glass. You can observe things in the distance as if they are within your very grasp!! This is a form of illusion, for you are here in one place while the distance is another one, but somehow it does not seem so!! You soon adjust to these phenomena and take it in your stride! In fact you begin to adjust your perception of what is real and what is a form of reality!! We do not wish to confuse you with that statement for the whole of reality is a form of *illusion* but it is in *degrees* as it were. You touch, and it is not there, and yet it is!! You will understand when you are actually doing this for yourselves. But to try and grasp this idea is most difficult for the human brain to understand for it deals with what it knows as reality when in fact most forms of so called reality have an element of illusion in them have they not? Think about that and then perhaps you will be able to grasp what we are telling you!

This new form of existence is to help you adjust to what is now your permanent lifestyle once you have vacated the Earth plane!! Your new world of existence is to help you to unravel what has always been non understandable to you. For the "after life" so called has always been shrouded in mystery for the Earth bound traveller, one day it will cease to be, and then this form of adjusting will not be needed, for you will be living it as well as living in the world of so called reality your Earth one!!! Which if you did but realize it is made up of many illusive qualities that you are completely unaware of while tarrying upon that lower form of existence!!

Just try and think of this realm the one you like to call Spirit as another form of existence that you have not fully been informed about, but which is a reality and is far more permanent than your previous one, for here there is no such thing as death of the body, it is just a transition from one sphere of existence to another and that dear friends is the form of deeper understanding and not necessarily a transition of the body, but the mind!!!

Too much for you to think upon at this stage of your development. You have to live while upon the earth and that takes up most of your so called everyday existence, but there is an inner life if you did but know it, where you can start to learn about your extension that you call Spirit!! Tap into this inner knowledge, and learn more about what awaits you when it is your turn to leave this mortal body of yours behind you and step into your new one which in reality is your old and trusted one that has been waiting to be liberated from it's prison of the mortal body of flesh that you needed while travelling upon the lower form of existence called Earth!!

That place was one of many that you will travel and live upon on your way back to the source of all creation, which one day is the ultimate goal of us all!! So accept that this next realm of existence that you know as Spirit is but the first of the many realms that you will inhabit on that long journey back to where non reality has no existence for it is the everlasting *NOW*!!

We bid you farewell!! Dear friend. Your day has just begun, let it be one of understanding and inner knowledge. Farewell and may the peace of the One upon High be with you this day and forever. Farewell little scribe Farewell.

Chapter 25

TRUST

October 6th 2002 12.45 a.m.

We begin tonight's discussion with the words put your trust in the Lord your God! For trust is a very emotive word. When we say we trust someone, it means that we have absolute faith in that person, we hand over as it were our very lives to the one in whom we have given that trust. And so when we say Put your trust in the Lord your God, you are virtually saying I give to you my whole life I am in your hands!!

That is what God is all about! He is the one who is in command of our lives when we hand them over to Him! We trust Him, to use them as he wishes and sees fit! But, and it is a big *But* how often do we whole-heartedly do that? We may say we do, but if we are really honest with ourselves do we really mean what we say? The answer I'm afraid would have to be No! We pay lip service but that is as far as it goes, for to give your life to God would mean that you surrender yourself completely and who in this day and age would be willing to do that? There are so many distractions that seem to the average person the only reply that they would be able to give if God actually said unto them " Give me your Life" at one time the Church as the representation of the Almighty upon Earth was the recipient of many souls ready and willing to devote their whole lives in the Service of God the Father, but now? The church as such is finding great difficulty in trying to persuade young people that the vocation that was once sought after is still viable to the soul in search of its Maker!! Look around you, and see all of the distractions that go to make up what you term your every day existence. The youth of today look at the mess that the older generations have allowed this world of yours to get into, and they feel, rightly or wrongly that there is no future for them to invest in and so they live just for today, and let the future if there be one take care of itself! What a condemnation of what is thought of as a civilized society! You do not think of your neighbour as your brother anymore, you look upon him as a hostile creature, either to ignore of to exploit!! Your people of the Western civilization have no real concern for those living in the under privileged parts of this world of yours! You give and then you take, and you take back far more than what you pretend to give!! Hypocrites! Yes hypocrites! That is what those in high places are! For their eyes are shut when it comes to the real reason for their so called generous acts of bounty. They look for some form of recompense from those who they pretend to help! Always they give with one hand and take back with the other! That is *Not* the way that God intended his children to act to one another, for we are all His children, whether we accept that fact or not! So why do you ignore the cry for help that goes out to you from your brothers whose skin colour is different to yours?!! They have been exploited for far too long and soon will turn their longings into positive action, action to retrieve some of the wealth that has been pilfered from them under the guise of business ventures, that were told them would be to their advantage!!! Whose advantage we say? Not the underprivileged for certain, only those astute enough to play along with their so called benefactors!!! Those in the West have much to answer for, for in the past the exploitation of the weaker countries has been done under the guise of helping those countries to become what you call civilized! How wrong you have been! And now you are reaping the whirlwind of hate and destruction. Your whole fabric of so called civilized society is falling apart and whose fault is it? We say that it is the result of your so called permissive society!! Permissive for what? To do what you please without thought of the consequence to others! Self! Self! Self! That is what is wrong with society of today. You seem to have lost your old values, of share and share alike, it seems to take a catastrophe like war to bring people together, but it is only a tempory thing for they soon forget and go back to their old ways!! Can't you see that in the World, there is room for everyone, and for everyone to live in peace and prosperity! If you learn to share with each other, not only your goods but also your *love* for one another, and we mean the universal kind, that is given freely with no strings attached!

God gave you life! How do you repay him for that privilege? Not by taking another's away from them or letting them starve, be like Him, he gave and still gives to one and all, it is *Man* who holds on to the distribution of that bounty! Not God!! Go back to Him, in your schools, your places of worship that today are mere shells of what they were intended to be! And most of all *The Family* for it is the family that holds together a nation!! And Nations can once more become families in reality and not strangers towards each other! Families have their differences that is to be expected, but they used to remain as families didn't they? Well today they just walk away from their responsibilities and start afresh somewhere else!! What sort of life is that? And what sort of example for those too young to know any better? Go back to your old style values of being a good neighbour towards each other, open not only your doors but your hearts as well. And that goes for Nations too! Your world can be a beautiful place to live in, if only you can learn to live in harmony not only with each other but with Nature as well!!! For your disharmony amongst yourselves spills over into Nature herself, and she retaliates with destruction that has been generated by the hatred thoughts that have been sent out towards each other. Do you not yet realize that what you sow you also reap? And the tares that spring up all over your world are the result of that hatred which has been festering below the surface for to long!!

We started this discourse with the words "Put your trust in the Lord your God" that can also be interpreted as "Put your trust in your neighbour who is not only your brother but also a child of God". Believe in goodness, for it is real, and once you learn to accept the good in others then you can start to repair the damage that has been done to those who you have neglected for far too long!! Live the life that God has *given* you, show Him that the trust He has put into you has not been lost, only displaced, and can be reclaimed and put to His use once more!! Turn back to *GOD* before it is too late. Not only for your own sakes, but for those who may come after you! And you notice we say *May come after you.* Think about that and draw your own conclusions!!!

We bid you farewell this night and may you find peace within yourselves and give it out to others in need. Farewell, Farewell and may the Love of God be upon you now and forever.

Chapter 26

LOOK WITHIN AS WELL AS WITHOUT

October 20th 2002 1.05 a.m.

Welcome dear Brother in Christ. We bid you welcome. There has been much speculation recently by your Scientific bodies regarding Space and what is contained therein!! That is, what they think that they observe! But in reality they see not even half of what is actually there! The planets and worlds that exist are not always visible to your Scientists with their lenses of what you could term powerful telescopic lenses of the mind!! Yes we have said the Mind for believe us they feel that their minds have created visions of what they term the Universal bodies of the Sky!! Your bodies of Scientific knowledge are hampered by their refusal to acknowledge what they cannot perceive with the organs you call eyes. They look but they do not see!!!

Within the galaxies that you think you perceive are countless other *life forms*!! Man is *Not* the only life force inexistence! He has Brothers everywhere if he did but know it! But Man in this present unstable state will *Not* be permitted to make what you would call physical contact with other entities that exist throughout your known Universe!! Man, that is Earth Man is only one of many varieties of that so called species! And believe us he has much to learn about himself before he can be allowed contact with those other forms of life!! Man tends to look with his eyes but never with the *inner one* which is really not an eye but a perception! And that perception unfortunately is flawed even in its present state! In other words Man *must* wake up to those inner responsibilities that result in an outward expression of so called reality!!!

Your *reality* is only a fraction of what is *Real*. You think that you have come a long way with your probes into the atmosphere, but you have been sidetracked by your own primitive way of thinking that *you* are the Highest form of intelligent life force, when actually you are very low on that scale of evolution if you did but know it!! We are not criticing you but stating a fact!! We are *observers* and nothing more at this stage!! Think about that statement. *At this stage*! You will develop, but you are still in the infant stage in the search for knowledge of outer space and what it contains!!

Life is there in abundance but is not always *visible* for life on some of your so called planets contains life forms that do not require physical shapes to be recognised as human like beings! Do you begin to understand what we are saying? There is more that is *unseen* than *seen* with your naked eyes! And that does not mean what it says!!! Mankind is not as forward thinking as he thinks he is!! If he were then you would *Not* have this inclination to destroy what you do not understand!! And that means *Each other*!!! Once you have achieved that state of understanding and learn to *live* by it, then you will be in a position to move forward in your quest for knowledge of what lies beyond the perimeter of your understanding at present. Man must look not only within but actually *live* with what he observes. And that means His *Spiritual* side of his physical body!! Think upon that dear children of the Earth! Man is not what he thinks he is! He is far more complex than a human body made up of dense like tissue!! He is made up of many *skins* of transparent like bodies of *light* that vibrate in unison and so they are not observed as separate forms, but once Man has learnt that this outward shell is but an edifice that houses these many other forces then he will begin to understand the *laws that govern* the whole of living forms of existence!! Cease to think of the *body* that you observe, as the one and only real *You*! For if you do not try to understand that you are not one but many, you will never be able to progress in the way you think you should!!!

Worlds are not just visible worlds of seen existence!! They are there and yet they are not!!! You think that there maybe other forms of living life forms in existence and believe us there are, but they are *Not* always visible!!! What may look to you as an Uninhabited landscape, is quite capable of containing not only life forms but also the structures that go to make up a civilized form of existence! Think upon that! Your realm of existence is one of denseness, and so you are mistakenly looking for similar forms of existence, when in reality yours is in a rather primitive stage and not the advanced one that you like to think!!

We come back to what was said earlier. *Look within* study your inner *vehicles* yes we did say *vehicles*. See if you can separate them, and then "see" if you can understand who you really are!!! Not all of these other *vehicles* of *you* reside upon your Earth plane!! Think upon that also!! But until *All* of Mankind thinks along those lines, he will never be able to understand the complexities of Human existence!! Remember, when studying humanity always look beyond the visible being that you observe with your eyes, learn to observe with your inner senses of so called Spiritual understanding, for that is the true life force that keeps the physical body in existence!! Your body cannot exist without its Spiritual life force!! It is that force that animates the body, but is not always understood by the layperson!! Yes even those of you who are the thinkers of your world fail to understand the real meaning of your Spirituality which is the real and everlasting *You*. Release that Spirit force within you and then you will really begin to live and learn what your life force is all about! You are all part of the life force of your *planet*, learn to live by the laws that govern it!! For there are *laws* as there are in the whole of the known Universe's!!! Laws are made for the benefit of *All* and that includes Nature as you wish to call the unknown force that is the life force of the planet called Earth!!

Once you learn to live in Harmony with that life force which is a reality believe us, then you will begin to know who you really are, not *playthings* of the *Gods* but *Gods themselves*!! You have much to think upon and yes act upon before you can think of yourselves as *Brothers* in the Universal sense!!

You are *All* one Brotherhood try to act as one, *live for* one another *not* against one another. Look for the Spirit within, that is the next *body* of yours that you should be able to see, know, observe, and yes touch!!! Let that one come to the fore, accept its teachings which are from the Higher realms of existence. Work within those laws and then you will be able to live your lives to their full potential. We leave you and bid you farewell for you have much to think about have you not?

Remember little children of the Earth, you are being observed and by those who wish you well. Farewell, farewell, and may the Blessings of those upon High guide you in your thinking. Farewell.

Chapter 27

SPHERES OF LEARNING

October 23rd 2002 12.05 a.m.

We shall begin with the words "The Real you is not the one who you think you are"!!! We know that that does not surprise you for you have been aware for sometime now that this physical vehicle of yours is not the one and only one of you that you know as yourself!!! Many people are unaware that they have more than one body in which they can dwell! Yes we have said Can dwell. For you do dwell in more that the one body that you know of as flesh!! Your next one is what you all term as your Spirit body and so we will continue to call it that for the sake of convenience! And clarity!! Your Spirit body as you know is less dense than you physical and so is able to live and breathe as it were quite independently from its physical counterpart. This other body of yours is a very necessary vehicle for it is the only one that the physical body can communicate with. The others who dwell in the Dimension of the world you term Spirit, they still remain conscious of the one that inhabits the Earth plane!!! Your other bodies are shall we say loosely tied to the Spirit and do not come into so called physical contact with your Earthly one! They only do so on very, very rare occasions and even then it is through the intermediary of the Spirit!!!

These other bodies are of such a finer vibration that to be in constant contact with the Earth body would mean a lowering of that vibration which would in the long run be harmful to them!! Do you understand our meaning? These other bodies do not dwell within or near the Earth plane, their home as it were is on the Realms adjoining the Spirit one and yes even beyond that one. *But* you do not *inhabit* those other bodies until you have proved that you are not only capable of but also worthy to do so! For these bodies or *vibrationary tissues* are from the Higher realms and that is where you must eventually return to, via these other vehicles of understanding. For as you travel to and in these Higher realms of existence you are becoming a *finer vehicle* of *Gods work* and for His work!! And so you must be of a much higher and dare we say nobler form of substance to be able to be the co-worker that we all aspire to!!

The gross body of the Earth must be purged of all its grossness as it travels from sphere to sphere, and in doing so it gradually casts aside all thoughts of where that Earth body resided, until it ceases to remember it completely as if it had never existed! And yet that Earth body is very necessary in the scheme of the *Spirits* evolution!! Think of it as the scaffolding that envelops a building that is being constructed. When the building is finished and is *watertight* then the scaffolding is no longer required! It is taken down, and work begins upon the interior!! You see where we are leading you? The body as such is no longer required, and yet it has been very necessary in the construction of your real and permanent vehicle that continues the journey of Life!! So you see though the physical has been discarded it was the groundwork that was necessary while it was used as the habitation of the Spirit!!!

Once upon the Spirit realm of existence, then you begin to understand why it was necessary for you to inhabit that gross form on the Earth. Now you are free from it and resume your *light body* that you have shall we say somewhat neglected while dwelling upon the Earth plane! Here, you will start your real tuition of what the true meaning of Life is all about! And yet dear friends this is only the beginning of all that tuition. You have many more lives to live and with each one you become nearer to the source of *all Creation*. But fear not, this is in the very distant future and much shall we say water has flowed under the bridge before you can envisage that state of existence!!

Each sphere upon which you will inhabit is finer and higher than the last, and as you shed each vehicle so the memory of that one is shed also. You are purifying as it were your very soul essence with each incarnation that you inhabit. Yes each one is the scaffolding shall we say for the next one, and so it goes on and on, shedding and re-emerging as a new identity but nevertheless always the essential *me*. You alter but you are the same!! Paradox, but in time you will understand! For the *me* within you is that part of the Almighty Creative force that beckons you home to where you not only belong but from where you originated from in the first place!!

The journey is long and sometimes arduous, but the prize at the end is what we should all aim for, for that is the prize of *Union* with the Creative Spirit of *all* life force.

This is what the whole of our various lives are leading us to! We are all a part of not only each other but of all *living matter*. Whether you observe it in its primitive state upon Earth, or in its purer form as you travel Higher!! Each sphere if you wish to call it that is really an inner perception of what you are travelling to in your upward/inward progress! Not all spheres are what you think they are!! They can be places of habitation and yet at the same time they can be forms of *non reality* in the bodily sense!!! Think carefully about that. The bodies that you inhabit are *mind forces* and are not necessarily bodies of so called reality!! As you *travel* higher your force of life become less and less *apparent* you are *reality* but not always observable as such!!! Too much for you to think about little children of the Earth! Do not worry, in the fullness of time you will know and then you will *be* what it is that cannot be observed but nevertheless is reality!!

We feel, yes we are told that this must be where we leave you, for this discourse, we leave you with our blessings and thank you for the privilege of being able to converse with you through thought. We are informed that we should say to you farewell, we do not quite understand that meaning but we say Farewell!!

Chapter 28

MIND TRAVEL

October 26th 2002 1.05 a.m.

Dear Brother in Christ we welcome you to this nights discourse. Now where to begin? So much has been written about life and the one beyond, that it would seem what else can there be that has not already been said? The basic truth has always been and always will be that as human beings we are sent on this journey of life to try and fit us for the even longer journey that awaits us when we have left the physical realm called Earth! This journey that has taken us probably through many ups and downs that sometimes makes us wonder what it is all for and even why it is needed if we are to eventually quit the Earth plane and dwell permanently in what we all term the worlds of the Spirit! You notice we have used the plural word! Worlds for in the spirit plane of existence there are many worlds awaiting us!

Does that surprise you little friend? "Worlds of existence" that conjures up thoughts of other habitations perhaps exotic and different and exciting, well that is the case for each "world" is different and yet it has a similarity to the last one! For "worlds" can be within as well as without!! You have already been dwelling in two of them while upon Earth, and your inner world the one that you term imagination, can have to some more of a reality than the physical one called Earth!! The inner world to which you travel with the mind *is* just as real as you wish to make it!! Does that confuse you? It is a *real world* even if it exists within the mind. For the *mind* is the mirror that reflects reality from what you know of as the realm of the Spirit! That is a real world make no mistake, even if it is perceived shall we say only in the sleep state! And here we are not talking of the state that you call *sleep*!! For *sleep* can be the gateway to not only the next realm of existence but even further than that one!!! If you are able to recollect that one, you would say to yourself, that was just a *dream*! But it can also be a reality of another realm of existence, just as real and solid as the one you call Earth!!! When partly recollected you will say that it was all in the *mind*, and you would be *right*! For it is the mind that is the traveller and not the physical body that houses it!!!

Reality, can be many things if we allow ourselves to be what you might term open minded!!! For if you did but realize it you do live in more than one world at any given time! You must learn that not all of reality can be shall we say "touched" by what you would call your physical body!! That can remain as it were almost in a cataleptic state, while the real part of you is travelling on the realms of experience!!! You no doubt wonder if these journeys that you take are of any use to you in your physical body? Well to answer that question it must be Yes! And No! The main object is to stimulate your Spiritual body, which will in turn allow it to transmit to is physical counterpart *certain aspects* of its journeying upon these upper/inner spheres of existence!! You do not recollect all of your experiences but only a fraction of them, and that is those that directly apply to the Earth body!! Without actually being aware of it, you are *learning* even while not dwelling all the time in the Earth body!! Man is a complex creature, he has the ability to *create* with his mind, actual places of so called existence to which in turn become *realities*! To him and him *alone*! But nevertheless they are a reality and can, should it be required be observed by others who are not inhabiting the *mind substance* of that one whose mind is the creator of that world of illusion!! You may think by that word that we are saying it is all in *your mind* and therefore cannot be real!! But you would be wrong, for all forms of reality start within the mind, before they can become a physical form of reality that can be lived upon and within!!!

The mind is the tool of the Universal Creator and has been given to Man to use wisely, once he has learnt that his physical vehicle is just an instrument of learning and nothing more!! It is to be used for the purpose of promoting understanding between the two worlds, physical and Spiritual!! For the two are really one and yet they are not joined as it were, only by the mind! Once the body has been left behind, then the Spirit is free from its restriction, that was very necessary while it tarried upon the Earth plane!! All the time you have lived upon that realm you have been not only learning but also absorbing what it is that you are learning, for it is that *learning* that you take with you when you leave the body at death!! Nothing has been wasted! All is put to good use in your next stage of the upward journey of development!!!

When you are dwelling in the Spirit World, you become more aware of these other realms of existence that really do exist in tangible form! And can be *lived upon* just as you have been used to upon the Earth world!!!

The *mind* is the builder of not only *your world* but others also!! In other words you are part of the *building blocks* of all creative life!! *Mind substance* is not only real but is the substance of Life itself!! When you learn how to control that force that dwells within you, then you are on the road of discovery, the road that leads you to the reality of who and what you really are!!! You *are* not only a part of the *whole* you are the *whole*!!! But that is a lesson that is in the far off distant future of what you would term your lifetimes existence!!!

We have to learn the lesson of being not only ourselves but others also!! You have to think deeply about that before you can comprehend its meaning!!! We come from the Divine creative thought of the Creator of *all thought* and so we are not only a part but also we are *the thought*!! Think about that!! Too much we feel for you at present! In time you will understand, that you are *creators* and not only a *creation*!!!

When you really understand the true meaning of that statement then you will know who you really are!!! And that is a positive aspect of the all-embracing *Creative principle*!! You never *die* as you know it upon your Earth plane, for this creative power that you are a part of, is indestructible, it is forever and always has been and always will be!! Wake up to the realization that you are not only a part of the Universal Creative power you choose to call by the name of *God*, you *are* that power!! You are responsible not only for your actions but for others also!!! When you understand that what affects one affects *all* then you will be well on the way to understanding the meaning of why you have been given this life to live, not only upon the lower plane of Earth but also on all those others that will take you back to the source of *all* Creation!!!!

We are informed that we should end our discourse there for there is much for you to think upon. We leave you with the thought that we are *all* one and so we say Farewell little Brethren of the Earth Farewell and to the little one whose pen hand we have been allowed to use Farewell and we do say Thank You for your co-operation in tonight's journey of the mind.

Chapter 29

IMAGINATION

November 3rd 2002 1.10 a.m.

Dear Brother in Christ, we bid you welcome to this nights discourse. We say unto you thrice welcome little Brother of the Earth we your Brothers from the Realms of Spirit bid you welcome.

We shall begin not here within the realms of Spirit but those realms that dwell within your mind! We all have them dear friend, even here!! Those realms or shall we say those inner worlds to which we go to either in the state of sleep or what is playfully called day-dreaming! These "worlds" though conjured up by the imagination can and do become very real to the one who is shall we say inhabiting those spheres! But are they real places or just figments of the imagination? Well let us say Yes to that question, at first they are just figments, but as you progress they become realities!!! Peopled by real persons, known and unknown!! Have you not wondered when in your dream state, you meet people completely unknown to you? You even talk with them and answer not only questions, but converse with them also! Well dear friend do you really think that that is all imaginary? If it were then your conversation would have to be very one sided, for you would know the answers before you even thought of the question!!! So what does that tell us? That somewhere within your mind there really does dwell another place of habitation. But what good is it to visit this sphere if it is not for a purpose? You will argue that dreams as such are so fragmentary and difficult to remember so how can they be of any use? We tell you that they are!! But not necessarily to the Physical vehicle that is doing the dreaming!!! That will make you think, well what's the point if we can't recollect what it is that we have been doing!!! Granted it appears like that but remember that you are not just one body but many!! And it is one of those others that the lessons are for!!! You will then say, how do *I* know that? Your physical body does not, only in a vague sense, and so you get your recollections all mixed up and what was a coherent realization becomes just a dream and then dismissed! But to the one who it was intended to be a lesson it is a reality and not an illusion!! With daydreams, they are for the body the physical one, they do sometimes include lessons, but more often than not they are just pleasant physical phenomena!! And are not real, in the sense of reality as you perceive in your everyday living!!

The brain is a very complex piece of machinery, capable of many things and when used properly are wonderful tools of invention and understanding, but alas, most people use their brain for simplistic forms of pleasure and rarely for creative enterprises!! Though there are the exceptions to the rule! Namely, the Artists and Inventors of your world of reality!! And also we include the thinkers, though quite often they only concentrate on one subject and neglect the many!!! The brain is the receptacle of the thoughts of the Mind!! It puts into practice what the mind is only able to instil into it! But once it has as it were been "programmed" by the mind it becomes a storehouse of knowledge ready to act when called upon by the mind! It is a "computer" of vast intricacy, and not only a storehouse but is capable of quick analysis of a situation that presents itself!! Your computers of today have to be programmed do they not? They do not think for themselves, what they convey has to have been programmed into them first by a physical entity!! So you see you are a wonderful piece of mechanism are you not? But why is that not used for constructive work and not the opposite as is so often the case with your so-called intelligencia of your planet?

We see the wasted thoughts that germinate in some of those minds, when with a little more constructive thought your world could be a place of not only beauty but one of flowering tranquillity. You have such great potentiality if only you can learn to direct your thinking apparatus in the right direction!

We started off with your inner "worlds", that in turn became outer substances of reality when used in the proper manner! The physical as you are aware is governed by the Spirit, or should be, but is so often relegated to the back of the mind instead of the front where its rightful place is!! When man learns this important lesson that he is the master of his own actions and not the unintentional puppet of them then he will have learnt that the responsibility lies within him and him alone! Teach your children to use their minds constructively and not as they now are taught which very often is to let them wander in their minds on things of abstract possibilities!!

Teach them about the life that they are to lead, not only in the so called "real world" but in the Real World of the Spirit Consciousness where reality is forever and not a transient substance that can wither and die in the wind of disillusion!!! You are creatures of wonderment if you did but know it. Each one different and yet all from the same mould!! Think upon that! You have God given abilities within you, use them as God has intended them to be used! Used, yes! And not abused!!! Your World is your classroom of learning to prepare you for the lives to come! Use your lessons to further your education that will allow you to progress in the Worlds of True Reality, which are the ones you call Spirit!! Think upon these things and think not only carefully but wisely. Your life is yours and no one else's! Live it for others but do not live theirs for them!! Learn to know what is real and what is not, in other words, Live in the world of reality that you call Earth but also know that that is not your permanent sphere of life, there are others that await you, far more real than anything that your imagination can conjure up!! Use that gift wisely!! Use the thoughts constructively and then you will begin to live a life of true service to not only your fellow man but to the Creator of all Life He whom you call upon as God.

We leave you now and give you peace and understanding!! From those on the Higher realms of existence!!! Farewell little friends upon the Earth plane farewell. May Allah be praised.

Chapter 30

NO MIRACLES

November 10th 2002 12.05 a.m.

Dear Brother in Christ, welcome to another nights discourse. Do not worry we are here to help you so just relax, we will do the rest!

Much has been said regarding your life to come, but there is always another facet to that life that needs to be explored as it were. Life upon the so called Spirit plane of existence is not just one round of pleasant duties, it really is not so different from the one upon Earth. You have your fair share of experiences to either get through or overcome!! That no doubt causes you to wonder what we mean by "overcome"! Well little Brother it means that here life can throw up as it were unexpected events that have to be as we have hinted at overcome!! You would not wish your whole life to be mapped out for you, would you?! The unexpected always presents a challenge to you, and so you progress, which is what Life is all about! And what do we mean when we say "unexpected". It just means that situations occur because people are still people with likes and dislikes, we are by no means perfect! If we were then our lives would either have reached the stage of Nirvana or would be intolerably dull!! You need an impetus to keep you on your toes!! So many people have the idea that once in the World of the Spirit everything is as it were perfect! Well it is not!! None of us can equate with that word!! We are imperfect beings of light, and always have been. Eventually we hope that we will reach perfection, but remember that real perfection is not lightly achieved and certainly not by us poor mortals!!!

The spirit world is governed by laws that apply to all known worlds of existence! One tends to think that the word "law" must mean some form of rigidity in the way one lives! But not so! For laws when properly understood are for the benefit of not only the individual but for the community at large. That has applied to your life upon Earth and is no different here. But with one big exception. Here you begin to understand why it is the right and only way to try and live a full and useful life!! You see dear friend, you are expected to be of use while you tarry upon this sphere! Everyone is expected but not forced to "to pull their weight", to use an Earth bound expression!! Life goes on here in a similar fashion, to your old one, but on a much higher vibration and so you learn to live not only with your fellow companions but for them as well!! Now that may sound all very cosy and nice and that is what it should be, but it is not necessarily the case!!

As we have said, you still have your likes and dislikes, and you might not always like what you are either asked to do, or even what you think you ought to do!! You are continually learning and that means just learning to Live!! That may sound as if it is a platitude! Well it is not!! Learning to live with one another does not come easily to everyone! It hasn't upon the Earth has it? Otherwise you would not be in such a turmoil as you are at present! You are still learning and living in this new realm of existence!! This is not a realm of mystical existence, far from it! Here you see reality as it really is and not as you think it might be!! In other words, you begin to understand that how you react to not only your neighbour but to situations is what is going to affect your progress here!! No dear friend, you are not continually being assessed as to how you are coping, you do that for yourself for you can see almost at a glance where you either have erred or what you should have done!! But then that is really just what you did upon Earth isn't it? Except that it took some souls a whole lifetime to understand just what life is all about! We are trying to get you (and not your personally, though even you need re-educating somewhat don't you?) To understand that life whether here or elsewhere is just a continuation of the previous one!! Different yes!! But still nevertheless one of expectations.

Please do not misunderstand what we are trying to tell you. It is just that there has always been certain misconceptions regarding the life that follows on from the one that you vacate on the Earth plane! We are not so different, we do not suddenly become Angelic like beings. There are those who are, either by the lives that they have lived or that they are of a "higher life force" from the beginning!! But that is another subject and not one that we are permitted to dwell upon at this stage! We can tell you though that you do come into contact with these Higher beings when you are ready to understand why it is that you are privileged to do so!! But by and large these other entities, watch, observe and are shall we say in the "background" of the ongoing Life upon this sphere.

We live as has been stated within certain laws, laws for the good of all. That is the pathway to living in harmony, not only with each other but also with what we shall term Nature, which is another word for the God force. Which when properly understood does mean a harmonious existence which if practiced upon Earth would mean the end of strife and starvation, and here we talk not only of the body but the so called Spirit as well!!! Think about that!!

Do not be daunted by what we have spoken of regarding your life to come. It is a glorious one, one that when lived properly can be so rewarding and uplifting. But do not expect miracles!! A miracle is just knowing how to use the law as it is intended to be used!! And we say that if that was understood in its right sense then misunderstanding would cease to exist!! Live within and by the law of the Life force it is there to be used, but not abused as is so often the case, yes even upon our sphere, of existence!! We are all learning that to co-exist in complete harmony one has to work at it, it does not come automatically as most people seem to think it does, once liberated from the earthly body!!!

This life that you will lead is to further you for existing ones to come!! For they are there for you to live when you are ready to do so! There! We do not want you to feel that what we have said to you is to make you unhappy about the life that awaits you here. It is one of great joy and happiness. One in which you can express yourself as you have never been able to before! But remember No miracles. We live lives of simplicity and that is not quite what it sounds! Think about it and see if you can understand our meaning! Life is a school and the school of Life is one of living!!

We feel that this is a good place to conclude this part of tonights discourse, and that means that in the future sometime we will continue where we have left off this night, for there is so much more that we can with permission tell you about!!! You see little scribe even we have to work within the law, and so when we are informed that it is time to depart, then that is what we have to do!!!

Farewell dear little friend and Brother!! Carry on as you are do not deviate from your work. We are always near you so you are not alone ever!!

Farewell and may the Blessings of those on High be upon you now and forever. Farewell and be at peace.

Chapter 31

OUTSIDE INFLUENCIES

November 12th 2002 2.10 a.m.

Welcome dear Friend Welcome. We your Brothers in Christ bid you welcome.

Life seems to be perplexing you does it not? You feel what is happening not only to you personally but to the world in general! Cease your worrying on both accounts. You are in no position to alter either! There are forces at work that are trying to de-stabilize your Earth and so far they seem to have the upper hand, but that will not be the case!! Good must triumph eventually, for out of what may seem chaos Will come stability. For your World leaders and yes your World populations, will come together and though they may not think as ONE, they will at least listen to reason! For if they do not, then there is little hope for this Earth as it is at present! You have got all of your priorities mixed up!

You do not Think straight, in fact many of you do not think at all! This is a testing period for Humanity, see that you not only profit by your mistakes but see to it that you do not go on making the same ones over and over again!!

Your leaders unfortunately are not men of High moral fibre or for that matter of ideal's!! For if they were there would not be famine and starvation and disease in your world!!

Remember the Bible and its stories of the Seven years of Plenty and then Seven years of want!! Plan for the future and do Not dwell on things that are past! The past is for the History books, live in the present and plan for the future of your children that are to supersede you! That is if there will be any to take on the mantle of adulthood!!! Turn back to the one you call God. He is the answer to All of your problems! For God is truth and truth does not lie for if it did then it is no longer the Truth!! Your schools and palaces of education do not teach the youth of today the fundamental precepts of right and righteous living. It is now Self Self Self! And where is it getting you? In a muddle like a ball of string that is all tangled up and needs to be straightened out before it can be used again!!

Your minds are like that! Jumbled up and what a mess they are in! Cease this headlong flight towards self-destruction! Why do you think your climatic conditions are in such a state? It is because you are sending out negative and destructive thoughts and these thoughts take on positive aspects, and they are not for the good of mankind but just the opposite! And those thoughts attract others equally negative, from outside influences!!

Can you not see the logic of that? Put your houses in order. Live by order and not in a state of wanton chaos!! The forces of evil are very strong at this present epoch of your Earths journey! But they needn't be! If you will only stop and think. Your priorities seem to be made up of Selfish Greed. Cease thinking of Self and that means not only the people of the earth but the Nations of which they are a part of!! If you did but realize it there is far more similarity between Nations than dissimilarity Look for what you have in common and work upon it, leave the differences behind you, until you can view them dispassionately! And then you will find that there are not so many as you thought there were!! And those differences are really nothing when you really look at them! Pride is one of the worst that you have to counteract. Pride in what was done in the past and is no longer relevant in today's world. Pride in the country that you live in, Pride is a two edged sword, it can be for the use of all and not to destroy those who you deem are below you, either in culture or intellect!

Remember you all stem from the ONE source, and to that ONE source you will eventually have to return. And what is it that you will have to offer to that Source? Will it be Love or Hate?? Think about it. You are the Masters of your own Fate, see to it that you are also its servants. That means service in its purest sense!! Sharing what you have with those who have not. There is enough to go round and then some, so distribute it where it is needed and do not ask for recompense!! The recompense should be in the knowledge that you have helped your fellow man to stand upright on his own two feet and not crawling about to find sustenance from the crumbs of the rich mans table!!!!

You have enough to think upon. Learn from your mistakes. You are being observed, even if you are unaware of it. History does Not have to repeat itself when it does it means that there has not been the progress that there should have been!!!

We leave you there!! And we bid you dear friends of the Earth, Farewell and may you receive the Blessings of the One's on High. Little Scribe we bid you Farewell till next we meet in thought.

Chapter 32

RESPONSIBILITES

November 14th 2002 12.05 a.m.

Welcome Brother welcome. You are wondering what tonight's discourse will be about are you not? You so often wake up and think what next? What am I going to write tonight? Well little friend no Earth shattering disclosures from the realm of Spirit we are sorry to say, just the plain truth as we see it!! And yes, live it!!!

We who dwell in the realms of Spirit are just the same as you, for have we not also lived at one time upon the plane of Earth? So we are just another human being who has passed from one sphere to another, and like you we were shall we say a little apprehensive as to what awaits us? For after all once the divide has been crossed there is no turning back, you cannot say, oh this is a mistake I'm really not ready to take this step!! Once you have made that transition you are now upon the next phase of your upward journey!! And what awaits you will no doubt surprise you, at its normality, for we just continue as it were our normal life, but of course it is not normal in the sense that nothing different has happened to you, for it has!! You have shed the dense shell of the Earth body and resumed your natural one, which is Spirit and no other!!! You have always been such, for that is how you came into existence, from the Soul downwards!!! For that organ is made up of many facets and the Earth body is the lowest form of them and as you progress ever upward then each other body is shed and the next one taken on as it were, a fresh garment, that has been awaiting its owner and is now ready to function on that particular plane of existence!! Sounds a little strange to you no doubt, for while upon the Earth plane you were inhabiting what to you has been your very own body and not just one that you have put on for a season!!! But that body is but a temporary cloak of identity!! It has been needed for a purpose and that purpose was to find out for oneself who one really is!! But this is not usually the case, for the very act of getting through life has taken up all of ones living, and so often one does not even think about what will come after when this life span has been reached. Well let us say that it is usually when one has reached full maturity that one begins to realize that this body cannot possibly be the only one that we will inhabit for the lives to come!!! Heaven is what most people think of as the next stage, and that is usually a rather fanciful idea of what to them is only a vague idea, of what Heaven really is!!!

And dear friends Heaven as you call it is still quite far away if you did but know it!! You are not yet ready to put on that particular garment that sustains you upon that realm of existence! You notice we say existence for you really do live and exist, there is no more so called death for your body is no longer made up of dense particles, but is now one of pure light, and please do not mistake what we say when we say pure light. For that garment is one that is made up of Lighter vibrations and they get even lighter as you learn to progress. This garment if we can put it like that is made up of translucent like elements that can be manipulated as it were by the mind substance that inhabits it!!! You can call it Spirit if you wish, but that really is not the correct word to describe that essence that is the real you that lives forever, regardless of which sphere you will inhabit!!! Now each sphere or shall we say Vibrationary substance is one of inward perception. No, it is not an imaginary place of existence, but then neither is it an Earth like form of habitation!

You are as it were part of where you exist!!! Therefore you are affected by the very force of the life upon that sphere! As in fact you always have been even when you dwelt upon Earth!! Wherever you reside you are affected by those surroundings, only on the Higher planes you are more aware of them and the influence of their effect upon you!! This all comes about as you progress! So when you discard the Earth trapping and resume the Spirit one, you begin to see things in a different light. But only slowly at first, for if you were to see things as they really are in that first new world of experience it would probably come as quite a shock to you!!! You have to adjust to these new surroundings gradually! And when you have adjusted to them, then you can begin this new life in earnest!! But remember, though different, you are still very much the same in thought as you were upon Earth!! So you have to learn what to retain and what to discard as irrelevant to where you now are! You have much to learn about this new round of living! No more struggle to survive, but still you do not just stagnate through inactivity! For you now begin to really live and that means learning to accept the responsibility for all of your actions and how they affect those around you!

You learn how to discard the feeling of Self and learn that you are now part of the whole and not separate from it! You are still an individual in your own right, but you know now that as an individual you have certain responsibilities and so you are learning to progress towards those other spheres of existence to which you will ultimately belong!

So, you see this next world that we call the Spirit World, is a training ground to fit you for those other worlds, for they are worlds of existence even if they may not appear to you at present to actually be!! You will find that life here has much to offer to you, if you are willing to accept it and its limitations. Yes we have said limitations and there are limits upon this realm of existence. We have stressed before that there are Laws to which we all have to live by! But they are for the benefit of all of us and once you learn how they work then you can begin to use them to your advantage. You will learn by the example of others just what we are talking about. That is how you progress and it is all up to you just how quickly you wish to do that! You will find that you have shall we say talents that you had no idea that you possessed!! Your life upon the Earth plane has given you much, but here you will then be able to use that knowledge that you have acquired and put it to good use to benefit not only yourself but others also. Remember, this is still a training ground and that means learning to live for one another and more importantly with one another! Think about that! And then you will realize that this next sphere in your evolutionary progress is but a step away from the one you have just left!!! To many this may seem like the Heaven to which they have been told they go to when death has overtaken the body, well if that pleases them, then let them think that, but to remain upon this plane of existence permanently would be a hindrance to Spiritual progress, and so they would eventually have to alter their perception of where they are and why they are there! Much for you to think upon little brethren of the earth!! But it will be worth it if you do. We must all travel this path and we do, for that is what our lifespan is all about! And lifespan refers to those that await you as you progress ever ever upward, back to the Divine source of all creation!!

We are told that that is where this discourse must end and so we bid you Farewell until next we meet in thought!

And to you little scribe, go back to your rest and peace be with you!

Chapter 33

LOVE

November 20th 2002 1.00 a.m.

Dear Brother in Christ Consciousness we welcome you, Peace be with you and know that we your Brothers come in truth and understanding.

First let us begin to say to you what is it that comes uppermost in your mind when you are woken up at this hour? You wonder why? And then you think what is it that my Brothers wish to talk to me about? Correct? Well first and foremost it is the Truth that we wish to talk to you about. For that is what we have to impart to your consciousness. Much has been said regarding life both upon the Earth plane and our world of the Spirit. And yet there is always something more that is waiting to be said. We say there are lessons that are to be learnt while you are upon the Earth that will fit you for the life to come, and you think " Well what lessons, what is it that I must learn that is relevant to my next domain of existence?!! Looking at it like that one imagines all sorts of things, and most of what one imagines are not at all relevant. But what is, is that to live a life of purity, love and understanding is the only lesson that one needs to learn to fit you for the stage in your journey back to the source of all creation! Now put like that you would think, "Well that's simple enough" But is it? How many people can honestly say that they live even one of those words that has been written? We are born without what is termed sin, and as we grow up we begin to see that the way people live gets them what seems like everything that they desire, and how do they do that? By selfishness mostly. And one would say can they be blamed for that? For living upon Earth seems like a battleground of first come! First served! But that should not be the case, you look around you and what do you see? Not looks on peoples faces of love and tranquillity, but tenseness and yes we will say it "greed". It may not look like it but it is there beneath the surface. We know that life today is very fast and not even sure, for what is right today, is wrong tomorrow! There is haste in everything one does today, and where is it getting you? Not happiness or peace of mind. There is so much materialism upon the Earth, try to acquire as much as you can before someone else does! Survival of the fittest!! But how often do you see that the mighty have fallen!! And it is the so called "weak" that survive!! There appears to be no justice does there not in your Earth world today. People are not happy even when they surround themselves with possessions and trappings of wealth, does it give them security and peace of mind? The answer is No! And why? It is because they have got their priorities all mixed up!! The simple life does not seem what they are looking for, and what they do find is far from simplicity. The moral fibre of today's populations is lacking, you are building your castles upon sand!! No foundations and so comes the storm and your homes are swept away, and that let us hasten to add refers to your inner life and not the outer one!

Where have all your true values gone to? We say that the source of all happiness is the Family! Yes the Family. Go back to when each member looked after the other members, love was what was the tie that bound the family together and yes Nations as well. For all Nations are part of the family of Mankind. Start to look at each other not with envy or hatred but with love and understanding and if you can't feel love for your fellow man then you are at a loss, for harmony will elude you. You must not think of just yourselves, for everyone is dependant upon someone, whether it be a partner or even a Nation! You can no longer isolate yourself. Your world is rapidly shrinking and so what affects one, affects all! You have got to learn to live with one another, cease this searching for what others may seem to have, your saying "that the grass is greener in the other field" is very apt. Look around you at what you have and you will be surprised. Wealth is not dependant upon possessions but is in the love of those near and dear to you. That is the lesson that is needed to be learnt. Love thy neighbour as you love yourself.

The trouble with your World today is that you do not love yourself, you are too busy coveting what someone else has, and you forget the treasure that lies beneath your feet. Love is that treasure. Love in its broadest sense, and that means unselfish love, start to look around you, smile at the stranger that you pass in the street, you'll be surprised at the warmth that you will feel, especially when your smile is returned. It does not cost a penny for love is priceless, it was given to us by the One above and given freely, so why not give it out to those who you call your brothers? Notice the change in your lives, and you will find that you really begin to live a fuller and richer life in everyway.

God is the answer to all of your problems, seek Him out in your hearts and you then will begin to live the way you know how you should. It is as simple as that, ask and you will receive of His bounty, but do not keep it to yourself, you are given it to be shared with others.

We leave you with that one word Love. It is the answer to all of your problems believe us, we know!!!

Farewell dear friends upon the Earth. Farewell!!

Chapter 34

LOOK WITHIN

November 21 2002 Morning

Take up your pen, little Brother for we are here. We understand about your thoughts regarding the Creator of all Creation! Do not think that you are in the minority in wondering about that subject. For it has puzzled great minds all through the ages and will continue to do so!! We are speaking of what is unknowable not only to us but to all forms of "thinking creatures." The whole concept of Creation being created by one single being that human's tend to call by the name of God, or Jehovah, or Allah, or of one of the many names that are attributed to the Universal Creator of All life forms! We cannot know, and yes we never will know. But do not let that statement put you off from thinking of that Creator as a Human like Being. For that is what the Creator has allowed us all to portray "him" as such! For we are but minute specks of that Creator and yet we are important to that ONE. Believe that little Brother. We are all important. No, we are not replicas of that Creative Principle. But we are replicas of that Creator's thoughts. For the Creator continually Thinks and transforms that thought into positive action, which has and still is resulting in life forms of many aspects!! Think upon that statement! We are living proof of that. That is All of the life forms that not only surround you but are there waiting to emerge!! We cannot with our primitive thought power understand the complexities of Creation! Yet we do have the capacity to partly understand what we are being told, and "told" is only a word, for we are not told verbally but in our thoughts. We are all individual and so we all think in different ways. What to one is feasible to another would seem not! And so we all "see" our Creator in a different light. And who is to say which of us is right in our thoughts?

That is not only the beauty of the ONE on High but in " His" gift to us of creative thoughts but is also "his" trust as it were that we will eventually become more like what has been envisaged by that Creator! We are but children, and children need to be taught and not allowed to go their own way. It is by example that the lessons that need to learnt are learned! All through the ages there have been these examples manifested upon this lower plane of existence. And there will come more as Man tries to improve himself, and how can he do this? By looking within! And seeing who he really is! Not just this physical body with all its aches and pains and ills that seem to be hereditary to him. This earth plane is a breeding ground, but what may seem like disasters can be overcome by positive thought and action. Man is the supreme life force upon this planet but he is also its custodian of that life force in all its many aspects. You follow what we are saying He must not only consider himself he has to consider not only those other life forms, but also his environment! He must cultivate a love for this Earth of His, for it is only on loan to him, for as you know it is not his permanent habitation, but it must be looked after for those who will follow him!!! And we speak not of those human beings that are Mankind today, but of those others who are of a higher form of creation yet to be born!!! Much for you to think about. Mankind as such is not the final form that is to be created!! He is but a forerunner of those others that we have spoken of! All part of the ongoing Creative principle!!!

There are others that already exist unknown to you who are also part of this human experimentation. You may gasp at that word but it is true!! We that is not only the human body but the

Spirit one also are all part of this ongoing creative principle!! The whole conception of Creation is so vast as to be incomprehensible to all of us in our "present form". We are progressing, but oh so slowly but nevertheless in the right direction. Time as we know it is of no consequence in the evolution of what we understand of as life. For life is forever, even if it is altered it is still life believe that, for it is the Truth.

The Creator can never "NOT BE" and so as we are part of that Creative principle we too will forever be, until the Creator of all decides otherwise!!! We leave you in Peace. Be not disturbed, we are all learning and to each his own.

We bid you Farewell little people of the Earth plane Farewell.

Chapter 35

LEARNING TO LIVE

November 22nd 2002 1.15 a.m.

How shall we begin? You have wondered in your mind just what it is that really lies ahead of you once you leave this mortal body and embark upon a new life's round of experiences? You have lived through one life's cycle and wonder what this next one offers you? Are you to experience what you have just left behind you, or does this new world to which you are now entering upon offer you yet more of life's trials to overcome and profit by?? So much speculation, and so much misrepresentation of what actually awaits you upon the realm of Spirit existence. You have been told that you review all of your past life, and then you have to adjust to your new one!! And what can you expect of it? Not a 9 to 5 job surely? You feel you have left all of those mundane things behind you and you look forward to what? Will it be anything like your previous one? And if it is? Well to some that would seem like a disappointment. But think about it! Would it really be so much of a disappointment to feel that this new life is so similar to the one you've left behind? For after all you have spent a whole lifetime of adjusting to learning how to live upon your planet of Earth and surely that time has not been wasted! And if it hasn't then what is the relevance of it to your new round of the life's cycle? So you see in many ways it must of necessity be of a similar nature mustn't it? If what you have learnt is to be of any use to you now? You do not discard all of those experiences that you have gone through, they must be put to good use, otherwise you might say that the time that you spent upon the Earth plane has been a waste! And that is not what you were put upon that plane for. It was to fit you for your ever-upward journey in your evolution of the Spirit! For first and foremost that is what you are! Spirit. A funny term to use for the true body of the mind that is the real and only You. So what is it that you have learnt that is relevant here in your realm of that name? You are still an individual in your own right. You always have been and yes always will be!! You do not suddenly become all wise and knowledgeable!! That, you have to learn! For your life upon Earth was a form of schooling, and likewise your life here continues your education!! Do not be alarmed, for all the time that you dwelt upon Earth you were learning even if you were not actually aware of what it was that you were learning. For life is shall we say almost a battleground of the senses. Right and Wrong, Good and Bad, it takes one a lifetime to yet understand what is what! It is not all black and white, there are many grey areas in between! You learn to compromise all through that life of yours. That is if you are wise enough to take that path! So you should have learnt that lesson, and if you have then you will start here with shall we say a bonus? So many souls come over to us, not having learnt that simple lesson and so they have to start with that handicap!!

Not everything in our World is shall we say "straightforward". That is your life here will be just as unexpected as it was upon Earth. But here you are expected to know how to cope with it!!! No, dear friends you are not in competition with one another in an effort to alter your life style. For here, competition is unknown! You live for one another for that is what your life upon earth should have taught you. But sadly in many cases that has been somewhat neglected!! There are many places in the world of the Spirit where that can be rectified! Those who have been selfish in the earth life are here shown how to live unselfishly. You are not criticised for that trait, for you can see it in yourself for yourself!

And so you are anxious to rectify it and once you do, then a wide vista of new activities are open to you. You are now going to learn about the lives that await you upon the various realms of Spirit! Yes, there are "realms", we do not all live or exist on the same ones! We progress to the one which is most suitable to our next stage in the development of the inner understanding of why we are what we are!! Each stage is for the purpose of advancing the Spirit in its many aspects!! Here you will have the choice of either staying where you are and helping those who are in need, or going to other realms where your aptitudes can best be used!

You may wish to remain near to the Earth plane to help those on that sphere, for those upon Earth are always in need of Spiritual guidance and that is what you can become. A guide, one who has had the same experience upon the Earth plane and so can uplift someone who is in need of your help and yes even expertise!! You see, your life upon Earth can fit you for various forms of service, for that is what life upon the Spirit realm is all about! But don't think that the word service means a life of servitude. Service here is completely different to what it was upon Earth, for here you give it voluntarily and with Love. All our work upon the realm of Spirit is motivated by that one word, Love.

It can accomplish so much and the results are lasting to all concerned!! You see dear friends your life here is what You make of it. It all depends upon your outlook and what it is that you wish to accomplish. You are still learning and that learning is knowing how to Live and that is living for others and not just for oneself! This may all sound very altruistic to you at present, but it is the normal way of living here, though that is not to say that you have to "get on" with everyone that you come into contact with!! That is a lesson that you may have to learn!!! You still have your own likes and dislikes, this is not Heaven yet!! But it is on the way to that place where we all aspire to one day get to!!! So you see, your life upon Earth has fitted you for this next one hasn't it? It has not been wasted, even if you think sometimes what is it that I have achieved in this life. It is becoming a real Human being, one who genuinely loves his fellow man, that is the real achievement of living your life upon Earth, and not this false status of how you can be better than the next man in your aim to "get on" in life!! Getting on, is really getting to know yourself, who you really are and if you can honestly feel satisfied with what you see then you really have learned the lesson of Life! And the next one that awaits you will be the fulfilment of those lessons learnt.

We feel that we will leave this discourse there and bid you Farewell and we hope we have given you something this night to think upon. Farewell dear Brother's, for you are our brother's as we all are!

Chapter 36

YOU THE CANVAS!

November 25th 2002 12.45 a.m.

Welcome Brother Welcome. We your Brothers in Christ bid you Welcome.

Think upon this, that one life is not enough to fit a soul for its journey of knowledge and understanding. It takes many such lives to even begin to gain such understanding! We begin as it were on a blank canvas, and gradually we fill in the canvas with strokes of the brush of life to try and complete a picture. One that when it is completed will be worthy to present to the Master! We are no artists to begin with, but by the time we are ready to move ever upward we have become proficient as it were, with this brush of life, and what happens to this canvas, when it has been completed? We are presented with yet another one, but this one will be a work of art, for we will have progressed.

Substitute the word canvas for a life span and with many brush strokes it is a life completed, and yet another waiting so that eventually the canvas is now something of beauty and no longer blank.

Each life that we lead, brings us closer to the realization of why we are here and why we are striving to be where we know we should be!

We have so much to learn and yet it seems to take us forever to learn what should be a simple enough lesson, that is: - Being a human being, one that knows that it is a part of the One creator of all!! That sounds simple enough, so why should it take so long for us to realize that, that lesson is all that is needed for us to progress? It would seem that the few years that we spend upon Earth just do not fit us for our long journey back to our source! The reason is that we are preoccupied with the art of living upon the Earth plane, and it only occurs to us as we get older that there is more to life than just living the way we do!!

And so we come back again and again, learning the lessons that seem to elude us. But with each incarnation upon Earth we are that little bit closer to realizing what this life is really all about, and once we begin to think along those lines, then it is time for us to "move on" to higher realms, where we then know why it is that we have been given this life force, and so we can then give back some of what has been given to us in the first place! Each one of us is a separate being of light and yet we all belong to each other if we did but know it! For we are all a part of this canvas of life, that is being painted by the Creator himself, each one of us is just a speck on that canvas but it is those specks that go to make up a brushstroke that eventually complete this picture!! We are important and necessary for this work, if it is to be completed and perfected as it was intended to be!

We sometimes wonder just what part we are to play in this journey that we all have to make, sometimes we may get a glimpse and then it eludes us, and we are back where we started, but not quite, for once we know who we are then we are on our way, even if the progress seems somewhat slow! Remember the simile of the canvas? Each brushstroke has to dry before the next one is allowed to continue with it!! That is each of our lives, and gradually we see that we are completing what was set out for us to do. And so as we progress even higher so we find it easier to conform to what is intended for us to be! We have to be patient, and learn our craft, and when we have, then we can branch out on our own, still learning, but this time understanding what it is that we are learning and why it is that we are doing so. Life as we have said is a blank canvas that needs careful thought if the picture that is to be created is to be one of beauty and not something that is but a daub of many colours!!

If you think of your life's span in that way then you will learn to live it in a way that you can be proud of when it is finally exhibited to the one who is the supreme judge of our work!!!

Paint your picture of life with love and you will be amazed at the outcome for the colours will be bright and glorious and a joy to behold. Each life of many strokes and each stroke goes to complete the intended picture that has been envisaged not by you the Artist but by the Creator of all that there is!! We leave you with our blessings and may you start a new canvas with strokes that are firm and positive and the colours radiant and true!!

Farewell dear friends Farewell, and to your little scribe continue with your life's painting for the picture is nearly completed!! Farewell.

Chapter 37

THE RHYTHM OF SPIRIT

November 27th 2002 Morning

Yes dear Brother we are here and we will inspire you to write.

You have wondered as many people do just what it is like to live in the world that is called Spirit! Well if we were to say to you it is no different to the one that you inhabit, we would be correct and yet we would not be telling you the whole truth. For though living upon the Spirit realm has many similarities to the Earth plane it is not over-powered by the elements that you have to contend with! Your storms and Earthquakes and upheavals, they are all a part of the natural phenomenon of the Earth, but they play no part in our existence! We have no need of such occurrences for here all has been "ordered" and the laws that are here are in no way similar to yours. Our world, as we are, is made up of much finer particles and vibrations than the Earth one. Ours is regulated by its own form of simplicity of construction! There is no polarity here, in other words there is no negative forces to counteract the positive ones!! Perhaps that sounds difficult for you to understand, for upon your earth plane there is need of this duality for it to exist. The pull and thrust of outside forces causes all of your so called upheavals and even catastrophes, which are inevitable with your dense and course matter substance. You are continually bombarded by Electrical impulses, which by and large are not even registered and yet they are very powerful forces, that were you able to observe them and conquer them you would have a more stable environment. But then that would defeat the object of why the Earth has been created. This goes back to the time when the Universe was as it were "born". Born of the thought from the first creative principle. The one you term as God! There was chaos, but chaos that was ordered and under control as are all things that come from the Creative source of all that there is!

Our world is made up of much finer substances than yours and so it was deemed not necessary for the turbulent atmosphere to keep it in motion. Ours is not affected by your weather or atmosphere. We have no need of it for we are bathed as it were in pure electricity that is something like a vast ocean of light and movement, but movement that is harmonious, just a gentle rhythmical movement, back and forth and round and round and up and down, but all in perfect unison. So that there is no friction from any area that we inhabit! And so likewise we are "made up! As it were of the same "substance". We vibrate in unison with our surroundings and so there is complete harmony.

That is why we are able to "come and go" as it were wherever we happen to be upon our world of existence. We are able to visit other planes of habitation by either lowering or highering our vibrations so that no harm befalls us because of where we are!! Our laws that we follow are for our own protection and good and so we abide by them without a thought. Now these laws pertain to our realm only. Other realms have different laws which are applicable to their life styles.

We are well aware of them as they are of us. There are many so called Realms of the Spirit worlds if you like, that are basically like yours and ours, but as we have said, Vibrations are what makes us all different. As you progress spiritually so your vibrations alter. You become less and less dense in appearance until you are All Light and shall we say quivering with life force an energy that is unlike anything else that you can think of. This light/life force is pure thought energy, not diluted in any way, and so it would have to appear to others as light emanations and yet within that emanation dwells the spark of the Divinity!! This is all far, far off in your time scale! Those beings that dwell there are ones that are and have always been, they have never descended to the lower forms of creation, but they are aware of their existence, and with Thought power they help when it is needed!! But not directly, it has to be channelled through all the lower forms, ours included before it registers upon your planet of Earth. Or others that are in need of it!!! You are not the only human like forms in existence! Think upon that and maybe it will make you feel a little more humble regarding your existence within the life force!!!

You are anxious to know just what it is like for us, and in time you, to live upon the realm of Spirit. If we tell you, you have no real yardstick to measure it by have you? But we will try and enlighten you as far as we are able. As we have said, here you are part of your surroundings, in other words you are affected by them and can in turn affect them yourself!!! But always in a harmonious way! Never conflicting for as we have stated there is no negativity here, everything and everyone is positive both in thought and action for thought is the father of action is it not? Our air if you like to call it that, is all made up of minute electrical impulses that not only sustain us but is also a form of nourishment when we feel we need it!!! We are what we intake, in other words that is our life force. We have no need of what you would term solid food substance. We vibrate with energy depending on what we wish to do. We regulate our intake as it were according to our needs. Therefore some of us would be far more "energetic" than others depending upon the situation! But still within the laws of Harmony!!!

You wonder whether we rest or sleep? Well yes we do, we do not sleep as you know it, we just withdraw certain aspects of our life force, and so though we may appear to be shall we say awake we are in reality resting!! Difficult for you to quite understand. Shall we put it in another way? Think of one who is prone to sleepwalking they are unaware of what they are doing and to all intents and purposes they are behaving somewhat "normally". But part of them is NOT there! Well we are similar except that we are fully aware of our condition!!! Does that help you to understand? We hope that when you think about it, it will seem clearer to you. Now regarding our atmosphere. We have light and warmth and breezes, we have our own form of sunlight it is there but shall we say not seen, unless you tune in to its "vibrations". Then you can see it in all its beauty. Likewise all forms of life force are there but not always observable shall we say to the "naked eye". "Tuning in" is all part of our life style and comes either automatically or with thought power. All of our life style is governed by that! Thought, it is a tool that you learn to use and use wisely! There are schools where you are taught how to use thought properly, and not wastefully. For here thought is energy, and must not be frittered away on thoughtless activity!

Now regarding Time as you know it. Upon the Earth plane if you want to get from A to B, you have to travel and so that takes what you call "time" either in minutes, hours or even days. Whereas upon our Sphere the form of A to B would register as "AB", it would be as one not separate, do you follow what we are saying? Our AB, would be a form of "timelessness". Time as you know it would not be measured in any way. We can as it were "manipulate time" to suit ourselves!!!

We feel that we will leave you there for you have much to think about and digest! We thank you for your "time and thought".

And so we bid you farewell till next we meet in thought! Farewell.

Chapter 38

JOY OR MISERY?

April 16th 2004

This is the time for reflection on what has gone before and how it affects those who are living today. Your clergy have just been celebrating your Eastertide. What we wonder has that passion "play" taught you? We do not see very much advancement on the spiritual level which would give us any encouragement that any lesson that had been given to you had been taken in and worked upon. Two Thousand years is a long time according to your earth calculations but in reality it is but a twinkling in the eye of the Universal One. So let us look and see what progress has been attained. Are you better disposed towards your fellow man? Do you express Divine love without any "strings" attached. Do you feel any real compassion for those who are hungry, poor, without shelter or a place to rest their heads? I'm afraid that the answer to those questions would be No!! Can you not see that God has provided enough for all? And yet most of this world is in a form of starvation and that means spiritual as well as physical. Your clerics have given with one hand and in the other a chain and for what purpose? To bind others to their will and not to allow them the freedom that was theirs in the first place. No one has the right to impose upon another being their own brand of what they consider is the one and only truth! Religion if you can call it that has no Divine right to say This is the way, heed it and if you do not you are damned! Does that sound like the words of the Almighty One? No! No! No! You were given many many examples through the ages of how you should live and treat your fellow man the one the Christians call The Christ was a good example of how man should behave when he observes the laws of God and not of man. For man's laws are flawed. GOD'S can never be for they are conceived in Love and Justice! Man's are not conceived but are contrived to keep the majority in ignorance of their real potential. Think on this, Man as you have been told was made in the image of God. When one looks at the result one begins to wonder What and Which God to whom they refer? For he has no identification with the real essence of the Almighty. Upon your earth you are surrounded by material possessions, hoard, store, do not let other have, that is what man thinks to himself. And what does this result in? Chaos! Yes Chaos! Man likes to think of himself as Gods creature but I tell you if he could see himself as he really is he would be ashamed to even call himself a human being. Harsh words you think? They are the truth. Man seems to have absolutely no conception of what he was intended to be or rather to become. For we do know that Man has to grow to even try to be like the God he says he worships. God does not require worship in the sense that you understand it. Worship in Gods eyes is Love and Understanding. That is what Life is all about. If Love ruled this Earth of yours there would be no more wars, famine would be a thing of the past, your so called Golden Age of yesteryear would once more be real. Mans idea of love is not giving freely but given with a hidden agenda, what is it that I can get out of this relationship? When Love is expressed as God intends it to be, then there are no "strings attached". You do not look for what you can get in return, you just give! Give! Give! One day perhaps Man will be in that position, when he at last ceases to think of himself but puts others first regardless of the cost. But the "cost" would be worthwhile because it would bring forth fruit in abundance. Cease trying to be "top dog" and look upon all others as equal to you, regardless of their ethnic origin. Remember, though of course you do not know, God is all colours to all peoples. Colour is just a pigment it is not the real person. Do you think your soul has to have a colour to show to which race it belongs to? Soul is from the Divine source which has no colour as you would visualize it. Colour is merely in the eye of the beholder. Within cannot be observed by the outward eye but by the spirit consciousness. Half of your problems no, more than half stems from the false premise that one race is superior to others. No race has that right. Only the Almighty can do that and as we know of His ways that would never happen. All are one to Him. How else could that be when you presume that you are in his likeness? Oh! Little people, think! Before you think! That is the prime objective but it takes a long time for that objective to be reached. Yes, it has been reached, so you see it is open to all to achieve that objective, but it doesn't come about by just wishing, you have to work for it. Learn, and learning is very often hard but in the end the result is worth it. We have not been hard on you little brothers, you may think we have, but you need jolting out of your present apathy as to what life's meaning is all about. Your earth is a training ground, yes a training ground for your own progression. Some have already seen the light and are trying to become children of God in the proper sense. Children can very often need correcting, not punishing but shown what is right and what is wrong, and what the outcome of those actions result in. Joy or Misery? Its your choice, not ours, we watch, we help when our help is asked for. Yes we too ask for help from the wise ones who guide us too. You see we are all learning, it never ceases, that is as it is intended. To stimulate within each and every being the desire to progress not just for themselves but for the benefit of all/ That is the lesson to be learnt. Not for the one but for All. Peace be with you my little friend, Peace and understanding, take heart you know you are not alone anymore.

Farewell little friend Farewell.

Chapter 39

GOD

August 8th 2004 Sunday

What and Who is God?!!! And who is going to answer that question I wonder!? I should think from the very beginning of time that question has vexed many people! And still we can't answer it to our own satisfaction can we?!! Perhaps we are not meant to know! And yet going back to the Old Testament, God seemed to be on chatting terms with various "dignitaries" didn't He? Well we've only got their word for it I guess, now you'll say "what about the Tablets of Stone that Moses had?!!! Well, what about them? Do they exist today somewhere? I know they were the Commandments laid down for our good and our use, but somehow I just can't see God writing them on stone slabs!! I expect you'll say I'm very heretical! Perhaps I am! But I can't help wondering, it all seems so far away and almost like a fairy story, if you'll forgive me putting it like that!!

What do other Religious authorities make of all that? I know that some of them have their own "Commandments" for correct living, and it all boils down to "common sense" doesn't it? So why do "they" have to attribute it to Divine intervention or inspiration? You must be thinking "he'll get what for" "one day and no mistake!!" Well if just asking for an explanation means I'll get my "come up pence"! Well so be it!! Anyway I don't see God as being that sort of God who can't stand any form of criticism!!! I hope not anyway!

But honestly, how can we possibly know or understand what the Creator of all that there is, or ever was, or ever will be, thinks or acts!! That Creator, I can't say "Him" because that seems too personal, though I know we all tend to think of God as a "Him" rather than an "IT"!!! All very difficult, because as little human beings we tend to try and bring every thing down to how we can feel comfortable with it! Though how on Earth we could ever feel "comfortable" in the "presence" of the Almighty is beyond me!!! Personally and this is only personally speaking. I don't feel in the least bit worthy of ever being in such an exalted presence!! I'm quite content to know that "He" does exist, witness all the wonderful creations that are all around us, that really should be quite enough to accept God as we think of Him. For to expect anything more would I believe be just too much for us to bear!!

So now I come to where I think we are able to see God not with our sight but through the One who travelled upon this Earth over two thousand years ago!! Yes I'm talking about Jesus! A human being just like us, but with the exception that He understood what God was all about, he tried to show us that living a life that is good and by good I mean towards our fellow man, we can become a part of God, not physically but in Spiritual awareness. He was endowed with that inner quality of Divine understanding that is given to but very few of those human beings upon this Earth. There are others, and have been others before and after Jesus the Cristos, and all with the same message which is Love one another that Universal Love that transcends the physical love that we feel for a loved one that we cherish! And even that form of love when it is truly given is an aspect of that Divine love that comes from the Creator, who through unselfish Love created us in His own image!! So that we as human beings could experience just a small part of what pure Love is all about. It demands nothing but gives of its all!! That is exactly what Jesus did for us, All of Us not just those of one race or culture. His Love though perhaps not always understood was Gods gift for All People everywhere. That love and the blessing's that are part of it are intended to Unite people, not to push them apart with various labels of this or that so called Religion!! God and what He stands for is above that and when the world accepts that Love is what life is all about, love that is given freely and is undemanding in its giving!!

Just accept that everyone is entitled to "see" God as they wish to see Him. It does not alter God one little bit, He looks down without favour for one section of humanity he embraces All of Humanity for after all we are all His Children. He is the Father, and we are His Family. We may look different, but then God sees beneath the surface of the colour of our skin, for to Him colour is but pigmentation, diversity of creation and isn't it wonderful to see and accept the differences knowing that we are All the Same to the Almighty. Brothers and Sisters, Mothers and Fathers, Aunts and Uncles, in fact a family, an extended family of Nations.

Glory in that fact, we all belong to each other, and what affects one affects all, see to it that we follow what God in our Hearts tells us. " Love ye ONE ANOTHER"

"In doing that you are showing your Love for Me!"

Chapter 40

MIND TRAVEL!

August 17th 2004

The World of the mind! And it can be your passport to the untold Worlds of Space across the Universe and yes beyond! For Space and Time are interchangeable and the Universe is not a fixed quantity but a flexible commodity!! In other words you are not bound by the imaginary laws laid down by Man, in his feeble explanation and attempts to get to grips with what is virtually unknown, that is if you allow the brain to control your thinking. When it should be the other way round!! Mind is the controller but then again Mind left to its own devices could become uncontrollable unless it has a Master and who perchance could this Master of the Mind be? Think dear friend and you will know the answer. Have you thought? And what was your conclusion? The Spirit! Yes the Spirit! For that one is the one that has been given jurisdiction over the Mind while it resides in the physical body upon the Earth plane!!!

And what you wonder happens when we leave this Earth plane for good, what happens to the Mind and the Spirit that together form a bond that can never to broken. So now you know that when we talk of the Mind being a passport into the unknown, you know that "it" is in safe hands as it were. Your Spirit you is in control, and that incidentally includes your physical vehicle as well!!! You may not always be aware of this

Union, very few people are, it usually happens when the physical body has shown more than just a passing interest in this union of physical and non-physical and desire's more knowledge on the subject!

That is when you are shown the delights of mind travel that can take you to the ends of the Earth and beyond!!! But you must be prepared to put "yourself" entirely in the "hands" of that organ of the mind and allow yourself to roam the Universe unhindered and unhampered by the physical body of the Earth!!! To get the best possible results of these voyages of discovery you must allow your Spirit to "take you over" as it were! Find a place in your home where you will not be disturbed by anyone, sit in a comfortable chair, do not slouch, but do not feel tense, relax, dim the light and perhaps have just the glow of a candle to penetrate the gloom. Breathe gently, counting if you like and see if you can visualize a black blank space in front of you, close your eyes if that helps, and you can even just hum gently to yourself. Let your thoughts drift right out of your mind that is the mundane thoughts of the day and of this world. Allow your Spirit to envelope you in its warm glow of love and now you are ready to begin your journey of the mind that will take you far and wide to places unknown, to vistas of such beauty and tranquillity, where harmony reigns.

Distance is no longer a problem for you are where you want to be. The blackness of the Universe fades, the Stars and planets are your companions. They, as it were, light your path to the very edge of the Universe that really has no edge at all for it does not end where you thought it did, it fades as it were into the space beyond what has been termed its perimeter, it is like a rolling mist like vapour of sound! That envelopes you in its embrace, you become part of this swirling vapour that carries you beyond time itself, and there beckoning you to enter is a light of such brilliance that you feel you must be near its very source. Gradually the light reveals a parting and you slip gently through it and there beneath and beyond you there stretches into infinity a lake so clear that you can see beneath its surface, a gleaming city, for this lake is its sky. You have reached the underwater metropolis of the planet Var!!

It is time for you to return there will be more journeys for you, as you get used to this mind travel. Your mind travel, Your inner World of discovery. Use your sanctum of peace and quiet when you feel the need to escape for just a brief period from this world of anxiety!

You can now travel on your own with you Spirit as your guide and protector. We bid you farewell fellow traveller of the inner life we shall meet again never fear. Farewell

Scribe! We greet You, we extend our hands in greeting. Peace be with you little Brother of the White Brotherhood of Christ.

Chapter 41

REFLECTIONS

August 26th 2004

If we have time to be quiet, and let our minds roam at will, what do they come up with? Holidays? Work? Day dreams? Life? And then if you are feeling serious Death, and what comes after!!! But that usually is as far as it goes! After all we are now alive, so what's the point of dwelling upon a subject that personally we know very little about!! But here we are just thinking in terms of our physical body and not of our "Spirit one", mainly because most people are completely unaware of it!! And if we are being honest, prefer to remain so!! Pity! Because that's the part of us that continues its life's journey after the demise of the physical body that we like to call Me!! But this physical "me" is only part of what makes us a "person". For the real person is that one that somehow seems to remain in the background and yet is ever present but not seen!! So isn't it about time that we got to know more about this other "me", the one that escapes this word "death" and continues where the physical body "left off"!!! The Spirit is the guiding force that keeps the physical on the right path. Though it must be admitted that the physical doesn't always heed what the Spirit is trying to tell it! Some call it "conscience", well I suppose it is, but it's more than that, for the Spirit is how can I put it? Well "its" a "person" in its own right! In other words it's the "unseen you", the one who you really are! This physical cloak of identity is merely what it is, "a cloak" that the Spirit use's while it has to tarry upon the earth plane which is not it's true home! This dense plane of matter needs a body that can live and breathe while upon it, and our physical body fits the bill!! And offers a form of protection for the spirit that animates it!!! As a physical identity we are preoccupied with its welfare and how to steer it through this life span that we have been given, almost as a gift, and so thinking about our Spirit side does not come up high on the list of priorities to do with our every day existence!! We have as it were, more important things to worry about! Commendable, yes, but there's more to life than what we imagine!!

So let's start imagining!! Why are "we" this physical person, why are we upon this earth in the first place? Quite a question, and to those who find this life a hard one, you can understand why that "word why" would be uttered with a great big question mark! Well the main and most important reason for our sojourn upon this lower plane is to be of service to our real self, "The Spirit"! "Well!" you might say "that's not how I see it, I thought it was the other way around"!! But in truth it is not! The only reason you, that is the physical you we are talking about, was created in the first place, and here we start with you as a new born babe!! The reason was, to "house" as it were the you of the Spirit that needed this incarnation for its furtherance of knowledge and understanding upon its upward path back to the source of all life, from whence it started on its downward journey of self discovery, to one day return with the knowledge of the reason "why" fulfilled. So you yes you the physical one are a very necessary part of this journey of the Spirit soul in its quest for the answer to this riddle of life and its true meaning!

So you see you have Spirit to thank for this privilege of this life that you are now upon! For without Spirit's influence and endeavours you would NOT be here, living this life, even if at times you wish you were not!! When perhaps you've experienced a bad day when nothing has gone right!! But come the next day and perhaps all is forgotten and this day will make you feel it's so good to be alive!! All part of your life, and it does affect that other you as well, you know, pity you can't be aware of how grateful that other you feels towards you for turning out to be what you are, so try and be in touch with your other self more, for its through your efforts upon this lower plane that enables the Spirit that is your higher self to progress so that when the time comes for you to part company as it were, your Spirit can look back upon it's sojourn upon earth through you with love and deep affection for the part that you have played in helping "it" to know itself just a little better than when you both started out together upon this incarnation of not only a physical body but its Spiritual counterpart, a partnership of Body and Soul!! You that is the physical you, will never be forgotten by the Spirit you, for you will forever be a part of the life of that one, your physical character has enhanced the one of the Spirit, so in effect you will live forever in that ones memory. Your life has been and is worthwhile, remember that when perhaps you are feeling low, you do matter you really do!

Try to think of your Spirit more often, and then you will get closer to your real self and you'll know that life is really worthwhile. For remember you as Spirit can never die and you as a physical human being have contributed to that ever lasting life. Be proud of yourself and thank God for giving you this opportunity to be a part of Him as He in truth is part of you!! Three in one you see "God, Spirit and Body". You are part of that blessed trinity! Believe that for it is the Truth.

I have to end this with the words Farewell and so I do. Farewell, and may you all receive the Blessings of our Father in Heaven Farewell.

Chapter 42

WHO ARE WE?

September 1st 2004

These are just thoughts that have occurred to me! They may not make much sense, anyway I'll wait until I read them over when I've finished them!!

Now we, that is this physical human entity have a body that is shall I say on loan during the lifetime of it! It is not a permanent structure that exists after our Spirit has left it at its death!! It will in time disintegrate, or if cremation is preferred it will then disappear completely. So that then is the end, the final chapter of that being that has existed upon the earth during its lifetime, however many years the allotted span has been lived! So, do you accept that this you will no longer be the you that you have grown to know during these years? You as you have only existed as a life form during this incarnation, which incidentally was for the Spirit's benefit and not necessarily the mortal body that it used, to gain knowledge that it felt it needed!! So now we know that we as mortal have never existed before this incarnation. What I'm trying to say is, this is our only existence, we do not "keep hold of this body after death!! We were brought into existence by our "parents", the ones that the Spirit, Our Spirit chose for us and itself for this lifetime of learning!! So it is the Spirit that is the only one that lives through each incarnation that it decides upon for its learning cycle!! We have our part to play for it is through us that the Spirit is able to gain the knowledge that can only be acquired upon this earth plane and yet is relevant upon the next plane the Spirit one!! But the Spirit as Spirit cannot function properly upon earth without its protective covering, which is our human body, that can function upon earth because of the dense matter that it is made of that corresponds to the earth's vibrationary force!!

We are a very necessary partner in this enterprise, for we encounter various situations and conditions that we have to learn how to overcome or even adapt to!! Now the Spirit doesn't always exercise control over the physical body, it needs the information that the physical entity acquires through all of these situations, without the aid of the Spirit so to speak. Though it can call upon its Spirit partner for help if it feels it cannot cope on 'its' own in a particular situation! Most people would not be aware of this liaison between Spirit and Physical, and so they would perhaps call upon God for help, which would be given through their Spirit self!!

So Spirit and body are a very close unit aren't they? And what the physical body "learns" is passed on to the Spirit via the "Mind" that the Spirit controls, even though we think it is we who are doing the controlling!!! So even when the Spirit "gives up" this physical vehicle it has been using, that physical vehicle does "live on" in the memory and thoughts of the Spirit who is eternally grateful for the co-operation it has received from its protégé!!

So it is the Spirit that is the one that lives forever and never, ever, dies. It may alter in its substance as it gets Higher but it is still the identifiable one it has always been. And now we come to the question of what does the Spirit "our Spirit" look like? For though for a certain time when the physical body has departed this earth and the Spirit is once more upon its familiar territory of the Spirit plane, it remains shall we say identifiable as the physical body it has been inhabiting for the benefit of those loved ones that reside upon the Spirit plane, so that the reunion of family ties that are still important, can be once more reunited for a certain period, until such times as all those concerned resume their true "Spiritual likeness" as we too do, when the Spirit is ready for that transition!!

Now back to "What does the Spirit look like?" before it took upon itself the physical mantle for this our incarnation! Would it be like the one who it was on the previous incarnation? Or does it resume its own original Spirit form? And what I wonder would that be like? For Spirit as Spirit is not beholden to the laws of the earth, the laws and so called restrictions that exist upon the Spirit plane do not bear any resemblance to those of the earth!! They are somewhat "Flexible" up to a point. Depending upon which sphere that is part of the Spirit world that they happen to be on at any given time in their evolutionary cycle!!! So Spirit can be what it wants to be. That is a visible form of identification to other Spirits of its acquaintance!! So it could be a likeness of a physical person that perhaps it was fond of during one of its incarnation's. Or it can be a manifested form of light emanation, somewhat like a vaporous substance, that swirls and twists in a constant form of energy which at its centre has its core of pure spirit essence that was part of its original creation. The mind essence of Divine Thought!! Cosmic energy from it primordial source. Ever present, always has been and always will be! As long as the Creator of All that there is considers it is relevant to "its" ongoing Creative Force of living energy, which is the life force of all created beings, in all spheres of existence known and unknown, seen, and unseen! Whether in this universe or one of the many others that may be waiting for their Creation to come into being!!

This form of Creation that encompasses many unknown "forms" yet to be created is so vast and complex and cannot be spoken of for the consumption of mankind upon this lower planet of existence. And so we must withdraw from this part of that little persons discourse who started this discourse on his own and we with his permission have taken it over and we feel no more need be said upon the subject.

So we are told to bid you and him Farewell and so this is what we do. Farewell!!

Chapter 43

A JOINT VENTURE

September 19th 2004

I have been wondering about the Spirit part of who we are!! As Spirit it must have been upon the Spirit plane many many times, and even stayed there during the various incarnations of the physical body that it chooses for each incarnation!! Well! That rather supposes that the Spirit would be well aware of all the procedures that take place when a physical body has reached the end of its life cycle upon earth and the Spirit is once more released from that physical shell that was its "home" so to speak for the brief span that had been allotted to its physical counterpart!! Now we are informed that once back upon the "spirit plane" there has to be a form of reassessment of the life that has just ceased and if there is to be shall we say a form of recompense to those who perhaps the physical body owes a debt too, it has to be worked out!! Well that was the responsibility of the physical body wasn't it? And as the physical no longer exists it falls upon the Spirit body to take over that responsibility for recompense doesn't it? Now as the Spirit was, shall we say in "control" of the physical body while it tarried upon earth, surely it would have been aware of what the physical body was "up to" and could either steer it away from any form of unpleasantness that would involve it in this recompense side after death, or if possible make amends where necessary while the physical vehicle was still alive!! So minimising all of this "going over" life's "misdemeanours" that the Spirit has to "take on"!

Now as I have said, the Spirit knows all of the so called procedures, so in effect it shouldn't need this having to "go through" the lifetime of its earthly companions re-assessment should it? I just can't understand all of that. Can it be that during that lifetime joint venture it didn't do all that it should have done do dissuade its mortal bodies activities that has resulted in Karma, good or bad? In which case were they lessons that the Spirit would have learnt and didn't? Which has resulted in this having to shoulder the burden of responsibility for the actions of it friend and companion who now can no longer be held responsible for those actions??! So all of this Karma business to me seems sort of "unfair" for the one whose actions resulted in it can "never" be brought to account for them!! And it's left to others which includes the Spirit to pick up the pieces so to speak!!!

Perhaps we've got the wrong idea about this Karma thing! Or have we? It may be that the Spirit must be held responsible because it chose the physical vehicle in the first place and so is equally to blame for those irregularities of the physical body in its charge!!! All very difficult for me to come to terms with. You would think wouldn't you, that the Spirit with all of its past knowledge of lives spent upon the earth that it would be better equipped in dealing with all of these earthly problems, surely it could foresee the consequences that result from an action on the part of its protégée and side track it before it became a problem?!! I just can't work all that out. Perhaps the Spirit hasn't got as much control over the physical as we think it has!! And yet the "physical" of say today, often remembers things of the past and that really is impossible regarding the physical body of the today because "it" has not existed before as a physical has it? So any recollections of the past must come from the Spirits memory bank and not from the physicals, for it hasn't got one that deals with the past!!! All very complicated, unless you accept that the Spirit knows exactly what it is "letting itself in for" when it is reincarnating once again and so understands what it will entail!!! I suppose looking at it like that, then there is logic in it and there is no unfairness if everyone understands the part that they "play" in this particular life's cycle!!! So really the Spirit is the most important part of this exercise in learning how to live a good life, which translated is a "God life". I have a feeling that there is a lot that we do not know or perhaps understand regarding when the Spirit returns to it rightful home and resumes once more its interrupted life cycle, before it can cease, this continual re-incarnation upon the earth. And yet without the Spirits unselfish willingness "we" that is this physical being would never be brought into existence, however brief the sojourn upon the earth plane may be!!! So we do owe an enormous debt of gratitude to our Spirit and so we should in all honesty try and live in harmony with "it", and not, however unintentionally, ignore our responsibility to its ministrations which are for our own good as well as for our Spirits!!! It seems we have so much to learn about ourselves and that includes those other spirit entities that go to make up what we as a Human Spirit body really are!! So much to learn, no wonder it takes so many lifetimes, and it can't be easy for the Spirit to have to keep coping with a physical person while trying to learn lessons that perhaps that physical body doesn't always help with as much as it should!!! I think I'll finish there and perhaps explore my inner feelings on the subject another time!!

Chapter 44

PHYSICAL AND SPIRITUAL!

September 23rd 2004

When we say that we have to come to earth to learn lessons and that we incarnate once more to achieve this, I have a feeling that most people think that when we say "we" we are referring to the "physical body", for most people seem to be pretty hazy regarding "their Spirit" if they even think that they may have one!!! But!! It can't possibly be their physical body that comes back for a re-incarnation because the physical body only lasts for so long on the earth plane, and when you die, that is it! You that is the physical you, has now ceased to exist, the body will normally disintegrate and that's an end of it! That physical body cannot go from the earth plane at death to the realm of the Spirit! It is only the Spirit side of man that can do that!!

So! Who do you think will do the re-incarnating the next time that it is required? Well it can't be your old physical body that no longer exists, so who then can it be? And the only logical answer to that question must be "The Spirit", do you agree? But because the Spirit is not able to function as it is, upon the earth it has to have a physical body that can live upon earth's dense atmosphere and so Spirit chooses one that it has carefully selected, before the physical has even been born!! So logically speaking this physical chosen body is a completely "new" one and is in no way anything to do with the previous one that the Spirit inhabited in that last incarnation upon earth!! So if by any chance this current physical vehicle say's "I remember past events" and then goes on to accurately describe them, it has not been what actually happened to this present physical being. It is from the "Memory bank" of the Spirit that dwells within that present physical shell! And because the Spirit's memory or Mind is now "linked" to the physical, that body thinks that what its memory says happened in a previous incarnation did happen to "it" because "it" can recollect those past events. It does not associate those events with the spirit that is now its life long companion. But the physical body is in error when it thinks like that, and unless you are one of those people who understand about this liaison between the physical and the Spirit, it will go on thinking that "it" has been upon this earth before when in reality it has not and can never have been because of the mortality of the human body!!

Now if for instance, when the Spirit was choosing the physical body for its next incarnation it decides to "stay with" the family of its previous incarnation, because it has an affinity with them and if there is a suitable "donor" and that is the one chosen, then the past memories of that previous one may have been stored within the Spirits "memory bank" and so this present vehicle that the Spirit has decided upon could well trigger some of those past memories as it matures, and that would certainly be a valid reason for it to assume that it had actually lived before and would not link it with its present Spirits companion, unless the Spirit decided to allow it, if it thought that it would be helpful for not only the physical but also for itself, for that might be one way of bringing the two closer in living harmony and understanding especially for the physical who would now perhaps see "things" regarding life more clearly and therefore be of more help to the Spirit in its learning cycle!!

I feel we have to think about ourselves, that is our physical self in a far more "open" way and not think all the time that it is we who are the important part of this collaboration of Spirit and physical!! We are, I grant you a necessary part of this joint venture but we must always bear In mind that is it "our Spirit" that goes on "living" when we poor mortals have ceased to exist and only remain alive, so be speak, in the memory of the Spirit!! And that should show us the right perspective when we think about this our life upon this earth!!

It is our, that is Spirit and physical bodies that are to learn the lessons that life upon this lower sphere can teach us, so that "our Spirit" can then progress on its planned journey back to the source of its Creation! Which we have been "programmed" to do!! So you see, though we are the physical part of this duo of the two bodies, it is the Spirit only that has this ability for "everlasting life" that is God given in the first place!

The physical mortal body is, shall we say only on loan to the Spirit and is replaced with each incarnation that the Spirit feels it needs for its progression ever upward!!! And it is up to the physical vehicle to do as much as it can to help further the Spirits progress! So though the mortal body only lasts for one lifetime, its impact upon its Spirit is invaluable to the Spirits understanding of the why and the wherefore of why it had to leave the safety of the Creator and dwell upon the lower spheres, only to find out its true relationship with the Creator and once more return with that knowledge to be a co-worker with the Divinity, so you see we do all matter in the scheme of things, even if we feel sometimes unsure of why we, as mortal flesh only have a brief lifespan upon earth and would dearly like to go on living as we are, even upon another sphere! Which we do as Spirit for as a change around, it is only Spirit who can function on the Spirit realm and not the physical body. It has played its part in this journey of life, and is forever kept alive in the character and mind of its true self "the Spirit".

If we can only learn to accept what the Spirit tries to impress upon us and try and live in harmony with "it" then we would find our life upon this earth would be more fulfilling in every way and gradually perhaps we as physical would become more Spiritual, which I'm sure is what was intended by the Almighty when man was first created!!!

I think this is where I will finish this "discourse" to myself and read over what I have written. Wonder what I'll make of it all!!!

Chapter 45

OUR RELASTIONSHIP WITH GOD

September 26th 2004

What exactly is our relationship with God? It seems to vary depending on which part of the world you live in! Here in the West most people I think, seem to look upon "Him" as a "Father figure" someone they can bring their troubles to and who will help them when things get too much to bear! But can God really be like a "Father figure" in reality! If you really stop, and think carefully and look around you at all of creation, the Heaven and the Earth, and the whole of the vast Universe that we attribute to "Him" do you honestly think a Creator of such magnitude could possibly be a "human like figure" that we can identify ourselves with? For me, I find that almost an impossibility and yet I "talk" to Him like most people do, and I call him by that name "Father" and I feel quite comfortable about it, and yet at the back of my mind I know that I can't be thinking straight, because I accept that a Creator who is responsible for all of our seen and known creations, just cannot fit into that category of a Father figure! So what is the alternative that can be considered as logical and understandable to us humans?!! Personally I feel that the Creator of this vast creation that we call the Universe and maybe even more, that perhaps exist beyond the boundaries of it, is not the one that we call Our God!! That Creator must really defy any description that we could with our limited intelligence and intellect be able to apply, to shall I say "Him"?!!! Our God?

And yet I feel that the one we have always considered as our God is very closely associated with the "creations" that affect us as human beings!! I also feel that there is an "hierarchy" of twelve "Exalted Beings of Light" that are part of this ongoing form of creativity! Isn't there something in our Bible that purports God as saying "Let us create Man in our own image"!! Well that implies that there were "others" who were associated with God and were also in partnership with this creativity doesn't it? So!! What then does God and "these others" look like? Are they all vast like creatures that perhaps resemble mankind but are really nothing like him as regarding "stature"? And just think of the "power" that they must generate from their "Minds" that must be awe inspiring when you think of how the universe and all that it holds has to be kept in check!! It hardly bears thinking about, in fact we can't can we? We are just not capable of thinking on that scale!!

Doesn't that make us seem so small and almost insignificant I was going to say "in comparison" but we can't be compared to those Higher Beings of light in any way can we?!! I'm reminded of those tales from Ancient Greece where they thought of the Gods on Mount Olympus looking down at man and then treating him like puppets that moved when they the Gods pulled the strings!!! Perhaps in a way that is what we are, sort of puppets, given life but with "no strings" attached so to speak!! But observed as to how we are "shaping" up, regarding what has been programmed for us!!! I feel that we have so much to learn regarding what our role in life is all about. Both as a physical human being and more importantly as the Spirit counterpart that is our true relationship regarding God our Creator!! The physical shell is just a temporary dwelling place for the Spirit. So perhaps that word "Man", when God said "let us make Man in our own image" really referred to our Spirit Man and not the physical one that only last's for a season!!! Thinking about it, that makes sense to me, because its only the "Spirit side" of man's make up that goes on living upon another sphere when man has figuratively given up "the ghost" so to speak at the time of death!!! And God is Spirit, so we must be, also if we are a part of Him! Not that I feel we will ever be worthy to actually come face to face with him, but knowing that we are a small part of our Creator and seeing all of His creations around us, that really should be sufficient for us, we shouldn't really expect anything more, just to know that we belong should be quite enough!! And I for one would be quite content with that, Though I don't think that that explanation will satisfy everyone!! Oh well! Perhaps one day all will be revealed to us, but I'm afraid that day will be a long time coming, and that is where I think I will end my little discourse on our relationship with God. Has it got me anywhere I wonder? Well I'll have to wait and see won't I?!!

Chapter 46

CHARACTER

October 21st 2004 3.15 a.m.

What can we tell you that will answer your silent thoughts? Whatever we say to you, you cannot possibly verify for yourself and so you will have to accept our word for it! Are you prepared to do that? Good! Then we can now proceed. Just what is it that we that is not only you little friend but all of mankind, just what is it that we come to the earth plane for? To learn? Yes, but to learn "what"? and how does this form of learning help us upon this journey of life and beyond!!?

People are told that we must learn lessons that will enable us to progress not only upon the earth plane but more importantly upon the realm of the Spirit, which is our true home the one that is everlasting! So how does this "life" that we lead, that is the Spirit and the "physical vehicle" that is our companion for that brief span upon earth? Just how can that life be of use to us when we return to the Spirit plane when the transition of the body takes place? To the majority of people just getting through life on a day to day basis is quite enough for them to be getting on with, without having to keep thinking whether they have learnt any "lessons" about living that will be sufficient for this continuing journey upon the next sphere!!!

Most peoples lives are shall we say pretty "normal", nothing very spectacular in most cases, so how does all of this "fit in" with what we are told is needed for our future lives upon the Spirit plane? Does what we do or learn upon earth have any bearing of how we live when we have left it, shall we say "for good", or perhaps for a lengthy period before re-entering once more the earth plane if that has to be the case??! Isn't life one big lesson? And that one is lived mainly it would seem by the physical being that we are, for this life span period that the Spirit has chosen for us? And what is it that living this life gives us that is relevant to this other life that beckons us? Could it be what we call "Character", is that what life does for us? Not only the physical body but also the Spirit that theoretically dwells within the physical shell during it's period upon earth? For nothing that we "accumulate" upon earth can be of any use to us when it's our time to depart from it, that is the "Spirit" that we are talking about! The physical has done its job and remains upon its plane of habitation, to disintegrate and be "no more"!!! So as the Spirit cannot take anything "material" with it when it leaves, just what has the physical body been able to give it that is of use to it on a Spiritual level?

Well? It must be the "character" that we spoke of mustn't it? Is there anything else besides this illusive "character"? It doesn't seem like it does it? For "character" is what is formed through "living"!! and that incidentally also encompasses the Spirit, for it has had a hand in this "character building" of the physical, even if the physical was unaware of its contribution!! So this part of life's journey that is a joint venture of the two bodies is a very necessary one as far as the Spirit is concerned. The physical body has been the "tool" of the Spirit, and a very useful one at that, for Spirit on its own could not function properly upon the dense plane of earth. So Spirit in a way is almost like a "sponge" absorbing all that the physical body is learning and doing, and it retains all those elements that it feels are relevant to this next stage in its evolutionary scale. The Spirit and the Physical are more than just "close" in this partnership they are as One, for what affects the one affects the other as well. Sometimes the Spirit manage's to "take control" as it were, at other times it has to leave the physical to use its own "free will", for it cannot override that freedom of will, even if when the physical uses it, it may result in not exactly "disaster" but it can come pretty close to it at times!! So that all contributes, to what we call "character building". It's how we react to circumstances, how we overcome difficulties, how we "get on" with other people and how we affect them and they in their turn affect us!! It really is just learning how to live what we might call a "proper life". Being a "human being" in every sense of the word. And if that means allowing our Spirit side of our nature to play a more active part in our every day living then surely that is a "lesson" worth learning for both of "us". Looking at it like that this word "lesson" can be seen in a different way, it's what life is all about isn't it? Nothing perhaps very spectacular, but being a good living human being with a positive Spiritual nature, that knows right from wrong and tries to abide by those principles, loving one another, caring for those who are perhaps weaker that ourselves trying as it were to live by those "ten commandment's", even if we can't always manage to abide by all of them all of the time!! And that also goes for those of us who are now upon the Spirit plane! We are not "super beings" just ordinary folk learning how to live just as we did when we too inhabited a physical body for a life time's experience!! So you see being physical as well as Spirit is important to the growth of ourselves isn't it? Substitute that word "lesson" for "living" and living is what life is all about, wherever you happen to be "living it" if you get our meaning!! And this is where we will end our little "foray" into the realm's of what we should all understand as the art of "living".

We bid you dear friends and that little scribe who is doing his best to keep awake! Farewell and God bless you all Farewell, Farewell.

Chapter 47

TO DIE IS TO LIVE AGAIN

October 22nd 2004 3.45 a.m.

This is not going to be a discourse but just quick thoughts to be extended at a later date either by "Me" or by my Brothers and Brian!! The thoughts I've been having this night are to do with "Spirit" and the Physical body that it inhabits when it re-incarnates upon this earth!! "Spirit is Spirit" and as such does not originally look anything like the physical vehicle it chooses for this re-incarnation! But it assumes that identity for the very purpose of identification as that human body of reference!!! Because it is expected to look identical as the physical body that it is inhabiting. But that is only for a period either upon the earth or back once again upon the Realm of Spirit. And "we" when we think of our loved ones of the family unit and friends identify them in our minds as we have always known them but we are looking at this from a "human angle" and so expect our loved ones to remain the same even when they have left the physical body and resume their Spiritual one, which has been with the physical during it's lifetime! But the reality is, that the Spirit the real Spirit is not like the physical it used while upon the earth. It "Spirit" is not a human like being in its true Spirit form, but we still expect our loved ones to go on looking like how we have always remembered them, and so their Spirit assumes that disguise as it were for our benefit, until such times as we have adjusted to the new life and here I'm talking about when it is our transitional period. But then our Spirit has to carry on with this assumed identity that it was upon earth so that the adjustment can take place. Meaning returning to our true spirit force that we were and still are, before we entered that physical body for the duration of its lifetime, that ends with its death!! And so we are then back as we were before we started that former incarnation!! Our true spirit self! And that would mean that the whole business of family ties etc will have to be adjusted, for in some cases we may not even belong to that family that was ours upon the earth plane!! So there will have to be a lot of re-adjusting on all sides won't there? But as we will all be Spirits we should be able to accept what may seem to us now upon the earth plane as a wrench from what we have always accepted as the family unit!! No doubt we do belong to a "soul group" and that may well be our normal family unit, but we should not necessarily expect it to be so!! That is something that we will all have to come to terms with!! And of course we do!! But we must accept while upon the earth plane that our Spirit is our Spirit and the body that is the physical one that it is using while upon the earth plane is nothing to do with us personally, even though we become attached to it emotionally and do our best for it while we are part of its lifespan, the same as it does for us the Spirit, even if it does not quite understand the relationship of Spirit and Physical. And let us face it the majority of people and here I speak of the Western hemisphere do not know a great deal about their Spirit attachment and only vaguely understand the relationship of the two, accepting that we do have a Spirit but they tend to think of it as an extension of the physical and would therefore resemble it in every way!! Which in reality is not so!! For Spirit was and is Spirit long before it assumed it's physical identity for the period that it expects to be it's lifetime spent upon earth as part of its education, for the earth time that it spends is for "it's" benefit and not primarily for the physicals! Which shall we say is a form of bi-product for its use, though how the physical "behaves" during this earth period of Spirits existence does have a bearing upon it, for it is helping in the formation of "character" that the Spirit acquires and takes with it when it eventually leaves the physical behind at the death of its body!!

So really this earth time venture that the Spirit embarks upon is mainly for it's own benefit in it's evolutionary progress. It respects and tries to look after its physical vehicle while it abides with it upon earth, but once it leaves it behind that is "it"! It is just a memory for it to use when it wishe's to remember past events that shaped it's destiny, but it cannot be expected to remember all of it's previous physical identities that it used in past incarnations, even if some of them were, shall we say quite important at the time!!

Spirit must go forward it cannot dwell in the past, for the past is just that, the past! Part of the now and forerunner of the future and that is as it should be, for that is what the life of the Spirit is all about! There may come times in the future when the Spirit will gravitate to other "spheres of existence" and those not necessarily of the Spirit but could be a form of what was once an earth life, but now on a much higher vibration!! That is what is called evolution, which does not only apply to the earth plane and it's inhabitants!! Contrary to what they may think!! For evolution is Universal in its broadest sense, by which we mean the whole of the known Universe and not just your little section of it!!! We feel that we will now withdraw, for your little scribe had no idea that this form of discourse was to take place when he took up his pen to write! And so we thank him for his time and endurance and bid him and you friends upon the earth, Farewell which we find a very peculiar expression which has no equivalent where we come from!! And that little Brother, will make you sit up and wonder!! God bless you little one, God bless you.

Chapter 48

THE BODY THAT HOUSES THE SPIRIT!

November 2004

THOUGHTS!

Thinking of the Spirit and what it means to various people! Those who are in the Spiritualist movement are well aware that we have a Spirit. But what about the majority of shall I say "ordinary people"? They have been told that we have a "Spirit" but does it mean anything to them other than just a word that is about something that they cannot see or touch and have to take on trust that they even have one!!! Well that is understandable isn't it? Those in the Western hemisphere who call themselves Christians are told in their Holy Book the Bible, that when Jesus left this earth plane He said "I leave with you the Holy Spirit given to you by Our Father in Heaven". But you are then left to try and work out what that Holy Spirit consists of and where does it live? Because there's not much room left in the physical body with all of it's various organs for something of an abstract nature called a Spirit to dwell is there?

So what then does our Spirit consist of if it's not exactly another form of "body"? Some doctors and nurses have said they have seen the Spirit leave the body at the point of death, and others have seen what they presume is the Spirit when perhaps an operation is in progress and the physical body is under sedation by the anaesthetic, then quite a number of people themselves have said that they have looked down on their body that is on the operating table and can see and hear all that is going on during their operation and can afterwards say with certainty all that they have seen and heard!!! And the Spirit that has been seen by others is a replica of the physical body!! So what can be made of that? The Spirit appears real and solid and not a wraith like apparition as you would expect!

So is the Spirit an "essence" that can assume the guise of the physical without actually being one? For not all people are able to "see" the Spirit even those who are in close proximity to those who can!!! Is that Spirit essence "invisible" to most observers and yet is positive enough to be identifiable as to who it represents??! To those with, shall we say a form of clairvoyant sight? Much to think about is there not?!! Well all of that applies to a minority of people when you are considering the majority of human beings. Now we come to those who believe in the Spirit side of our physical body and those are, as we have said, that usually belong to the Spiritualist movement and so understand more about the Spirit and its connection with our physical body during its lifetime upon earth. They know that when its time for the physical to cease it's life upon earth then the spirit is released from its habitation of that body, and what then does it take with it that the physical has been part of during it's life span? It is the Mind essence. That storehouse of memories past and present and yes that will also be of the future as well!! For without the knowledge of the past the future could well be a blank canvas!! So our Spirit is the most important part of our whole being is it not? It is the "part" that existed before the incarnation of this it's former human counterpart in it's evolutionary cycle. That is the Spirit's, for the physical body no longer exists as once it did! Any yet what it contributed to it's Spirit's companion upon earth has not been lost for the memory of that part association is still very much alive within the Mind and thoughts that are a vital part of the Spirit's advancement, in it's search for it's true identity, that will, one day, bring it face to face with its Soul Creator, for the Soul is an aspect of the one who you know as The God Creator of all that there is! The Soul is the visible part of the God Creator, that will return to the source of its creation, knowing who it is and who it will always be and can now be counted as a co-worker in God's Eternal Universe of on-going Creativity!

That is the prime objective of the Soul and the Spirit aspects that it has been allowed to create in its search for the knowledge that will promote it in its evolutionary progress. There is much for us to try and understand about the relationship between the physical body and the Spirit essence that guides it during its brief life span upon earth. It may be brief, but it is still very important to the Spirit's understanding. So even if we the human side of this joint venture upon life's pathways are here only temporarily we do matter to the Spirit, for without this joining of the two forces, the Spirit would be that much poorer and could not then evolve as it should!

Life may at times seem very complex, but once you understand that you do have a strong relationship with your Spirit and accept the advice that it imparts to you via your "conscience" then you will find that your life upon earth makes far more sense than you had previously thought! Just understand that you that is the physical you are upon the earth for such a brief period, it cannot be permanent for age usually overtakes the human body and brings it's life span to a close. And so that means that the Spirit is now released from its human bondage and can return to its true home upon the realm of the Spirit. But it never cease's to be grateful to that life long companion that was so important to it while they both tarried upon the earth.

And here is where we feel that we will bring this discourse to a close. In spite of the fact that your little scribe thought that it was his thoughts that he was voicing!! And so we must give him credit for his part in this mental discussion!!

And we say to you dear friends upon the earth Farewell and God's blessings be with you now and in the days to come. To you little Brother Scribe we bid you a fond Farewell and thank you for your co-operation and we will meet again on the pages of this your journal. Farewell and God bless you.

Chapter 49

THE WHITE BROTHERHOOD

November 22nd 2004 1.10 a.m.

Welcome dear Brother we bid you welcome in the name of Jesus the Christ, Our teacher and Saviour in His name we welcome you and in His name we are here to teach you.

You have "asked" about our life upon the "Spiritual Plane". This we can tell you from our own experience, though we no longer "dwell" upon that particular sphere. As you are already aware our "home" as it were is beyond the next plane up from your earth one, we have of course "passed through" that plane, in fact we dwelt upon it for some considerable time, while we were being "taught" as you are being. We say "we" though "we" were not altogether at the same time. The Brotherhood is "made up" of many of us and so we are not always in the same category, for example "I" may have been on the Spiritual plane at one time and some of my Brothers were on different ones and yet we "come together" when there is "work to be done" either on your sphere or on others. Like your various nationalities we are the same "here", so you see we are no different than you are in that respect. We differ in as much as that we "vibrate" at a much higher level, and with each "incarnation" for we will call it that, so the vibration gets higher and higher, with more and more knowledge we need to be very very "flexible" for our "work" covers many different "spheres" your earth included.

"Life" for we will continue to call it that, goes on in very many different aspects. We as your many teachers are just as varied as those in your public schools. The Brotherhood is just what it says it is. A band of like minded and dedicated individuals from many races with a particular "bent" for teaching and trying to impart the knowledge that we have been privileged to have been given by those who teach "us"! Each one of us is "hand picked" as it were, we have been studied not only while upon the earth plane and "others" and we are still being assessed as to our qualifications. So you see little Brother you are a "member" of a very special band of "beings". I use the word advisedly for "beings" should inform you that we are not all of the same "race" or colour or even "look alike" if you can get the meaning that I am conveying!

Brotherhood means "variety" but all with the same desire and that is to be "servants" in the cause of teaching what we have been taught. We do not "stay" in any one sphere "permanently" for we are called to various "places" when we are needed, that is our "work" and our "calling" for we are "called", and we dedicate ourselves to that particular brand of "calling". We use that word to denote not only our form of teaching for "teaching" comes in many forms, not just in the classroom!! We "live" our work, though "work" is not the correct word that denotes our form of activity. How can we put it that you can understand you upon the earth while young desire to do a "job of work", that is to provide you with a "living". We do a "job of work" not for a living but because we desire to be of "service" to others, and this form of "service" is what we have been "trained" for. We are "volunteers" in every sense of the word.

Now you have an idea of why we are called the "White Brotherhood" that really is just a word to denote who we are for we are "brothers of light", and "white" is the equivalent word for "light"!! "light" is how we live, and how we work, it is through the "vibration of light" that our whole existence is manifested! We that is you upon earth as well as on the other Planets are all "creatures of light" for "light" is the life force that enables us to live and work in all circumstances! Light is a "substance" that can be manipulated in any way that we desire. It is how we are able to "transform" ourselves to fit the environment that we find ourselves in at any given moment "light waves" "make up" all substances, wherever there is "life". "Light vibrates" and can be formed into what is needed, but "light" cannot be used for any form of "idle being". It is a "tool" that we are taught how to "use" and that takes "time" it does not come about automatically as some may think. You see little friend, we are always learning and being taught and then teaching. Our knowledge which we endeavour to "pass on" has to be given to us before we are in a position to call ourselves "teachers". Take heart little one, and do not be "daunted" you will see when you "come over" to us just how much you have learnt, even though you may feel "what is it that I have learnt"? You are here are you not? That should give you an answer to your question!!! Think, little one, think! We are not only your teachers and friends we are indeed your Brothers in every sense of the word!! You have been part of our Brotherhood for a very long time, granted, on "probation" as it were but now a member who can be called "Brother in Christ". You have earned that title, but it carries with it a great responsibly for what you "say" to others must always be the Truth and that is a great responsibility for one to undertake. Persevere dear Brother, you are "doing well". The path seems lonely to you, but believe me it is the only path for one who intends to be a "servant" and not a "master". For the greatest "servant" of all, showed us the way and still does and will do for ever for The Brotherhood is the Brotherhood of Christ no les, so you see little brother, you are in "good" company!!!

More will be given to you in due course, for now this is sufficient, you still feel you have not been told what you wanted to know, all in "good time", all in good time!!

Farewell little Brother we watch over and care for you both, be sure of that. Our blessing be upon you. Farewell.

Allah be praised!

Chapter 50

OUR OTHER SELVES!

November 21st 2004 1.00 a.m.

We talk about our Spirit, but what do we really know about it? And is our Spirit, our only one? Or are there others that we know nothing about? And if there are, what are they doing? And more importantly where are they?

We seem to concentrate on the next realm "up" from this our world, but are there other realms that exist in this our spiral of evolution? Words! Words! Words! But what do they mean if we do not know anything about these other realms are they realities? Or just thoughts that our mind plays with? In the hope that somehow we may stumble upon these other realms of existence?!

But let us assume that they do actually exist and that we that is our other spirit entities really do dwell upon them, and for what purpose? We know that the world we always think of as the Spirit one, is a real world, that does exist because our loved ones and friends are "there" and travel back and forth to this physical one while keeping in touch with us who remain, even though most if not all of us never actually "see" them, even if we may feel their presence around us at certain times!! And if it wasn't for clairvoyant mediums who can give us proof of their identity we perhaps would never know of their continued existence. Fortunately those of us who accept the Spiritualistic way of life do know of the reality of their continuation of their life's cycle, but the majority of people are somewhat ignorant of this state of affairs and would take a lot of convincing to the contrary, without actual physical proof, which as we know is somewhat difficult to come by!!

So what on earth would they make of it, if they were to be told that we have not one, not even two, but even more Spirit counterparts that make up who we really are!! And even some of us, shall we say "enlightened ones" have a real difficulty in accepting, what has been said!! For proof, positive proof, is not always forth coming is it? For the dimensions upon which those other facets of our Spirit "body" dwell are beyond not only our understanding, but can actually stretch our credulity to it's very limit!! We have to take all that is said on trust!! Which sometimes can be very difficult, when perhaps we are told of our other Spirit "essences", which to us is just a "word" that tells us nothing of what an essence is made of!!

If we are informed of our "Spirit essence of light" we can't really imagine what that sentence actually means! "A Spirit Essence of light". We upon the physical realm of existence are not likely to ever encounter, that part of our being, until we are back upon the Spirit plane that adjoins this physical one!! And yet that "essence", that "being", is part of us and yes "knows" of our existence, and actually does impress us with those higher thoughts that we sometimes get and wonder where they came from!!! And that is just one of our other "selves". But not all of them are shall we say of a physical form of identification!! "Some" are in a form of "silent slumber" awaiting our return upon the upward journey back to our Creative Source!! For these other planes which are other dimensions, we have been on before, when we were first created by our Soul for the purpose of it gaining knowledge of its true identity and to gain that experience, it is allowed to create these various aspects of itself, who because of their fluidity of structure can manifest upon the lower spheres of existence where the Soul could not venture! These "aspects" are not only Spirit essences, but also mind essences as well! They are thought made manifest, each one finer than the last, that is the finest starting from the Soul essence and going down the scale so to speak until they reach the One Spirit that is the guiding force of the physical body. Which is the lowest one on that scale we mentioned!! They are all "linked" by thought and those that are "active" can influence others and can in their turn be influenced likewise! So all of the experience's that are being collated by the various aspects will eventually find their way back to the Soul essence for its assessment! A long, long, journey of discovery we have to tell you, but that is how it has been "programmed"!! It may all sound rather complicated, but it isn't really it is quite straightforward in it's simplicity of construction and achievement!!

Each realm or sphere where the various aspects of the Soul essence vibrate are governed by the "keepers" of that particular area of thought. They are the Higher teachers of light, they give illumination to the mind essence of each individual aspect under their protection. They monitor the progress and when they deem that that particular aspect is ready they then allow it to proceed upon its allotted sphere where it can "join up" in thought with its other counterpart's, that are upon their spheres of evolvement!

They each remain upon their allotted spheres but are in communication with each other, but in strict rotation, for example one can communicate with the one below it and in turn be communicated by the one above it, but only by thought waves and not by shall we say "physical contact". That will all come later when the Spirit that is the guiding force of the earth body is upon its upward journey back to its Soul source. And each aspect will then come together as each one is amalgamated with its fellow Spirit, to emerge upon the Soul plane as One complete entity ready to be assimilated into the perfect Soul essence, that can then proceed upon the final journey that will bring it back to its prime creative source of life. Namely The God head of all creation, that is under the jurisdiction of the Supreme Creator of all known Phenomena that is known as the Universal Cosmic Life Force. The beginning and the end the Alpha and the Omega. The

Eternal One that is forever and always has been!!! And always will be!!!

And here we leave you after this nights discourse!! So we bid you fellow travellers upon the earth, Farewell!

And to you Brother Scribe we give you our Blessings and our love Farewell little friend Farewell.

Chapter 51

NATURE!!

January 11th 2005 3.55 a.m.

How can we greet you little Brother? So much misery that surrounds your earth at this present time. We too, are experiencing it as well for we upon the Spirit plane have been overwhelmed by the devastation that has seen so many many Souls snatched from life upon the earth and we must try to alleviate some of the trauma that has caused them such bewilderment and heartache, that has affected both East and West and the after math of this catastrophe will leave a scar upon Mankind that will probably remain for the rest of earths cycle of evolution. And yet, from out of this natural but seemingly unnatural occurrence of Nature there is growing a bond of comradeship that between peoples of so many nationalities can only result in a better understanding of how fragile life can be on this planet for not just one section of its population but for all of them!

You are witnessing a tremendous upsurge of universal love that joins all Nations together and just for a brief period they become united in their efforts of succour for the victims of those continents that have experienced this devastating blow to their whole way of life, which is some cases will never be the same again. But we tell you, that these scars and open wounds will heal and though they may leave a feeling of helplessness at Natures awesome power, gradually these tragic memories will begin to fade, for Mankind is a very resilient creature in the face of adversity. But do not let him become complacent for we are afraid that there will be more acts of devastation affecting the life of your planet, and this present one must not be thought of as a "one off", for sadly it is Not. Your earth at present is going through a complete change, some would say a cleansing from within as well as from without. It is inevitable taking into consideration the make up of your planet, which is of dense matter that is inherently unstable and has to periodically let of steam for if it did not, then your world would cease to be a viable place of habitation for Man, in fact of all living creatures, great and small!!! There have always been catastrophes in your world and here we speak of those of Nature, and not those man-made ones that also have devastating effects upon the unsuspecting populations in various parts of your planet. Namely those wars that you somehow seem unable to get away from, and all because of so called power struggles, that only result is misery, death and starvation, which in turn affects the very fabric of your earth!

One thing leads to another and results in waste. Waste of manpower and the loss of unborn generations and all because of Greed. You must all learn to try and live together in harmony, and that goes for living with Nature as well! She can be a willing servant, but a cruel mistress when you upset her. Care for your planet, for it is your only home that you have to live upon, you cannot "up sticks" and move on for you have nowhere else to move to have you? This terrible event that you call "Tsunami" is unfortunately a natural phenomena that you have to live and cope with at various times, you must try and prepare yourselves for these and other events that Nature springs upon you, learn from them, and do not build upon those "faults" that you know exist beneath the surface of your planet. Your whole weather cycle is changing prior to what will occur to your world in the coming future!! We do not wish to alarm you unduly, but this cycle will have to run its course before stability is restored to your earth.

Learn that nothing can be considered as permanent upon this dense planet of yours, and try and plan ahead with this in mind!! Don't build high buildings that can topple over when the earth starts to move, and keep away from low lying areas where the sea can engulf them and also rain floods that swell your rivers to breaking point. Stop this slaughter of your forests which results in earth that gets washed away because it cannot cope with the excess water, that goes over it instead of in it, causing these dreadful mud slides that engulf whole villages and their populations!!! ||Nature must not be looked upon as your enemy, you must learn how to live with her and tame her when you can!!

Look back at history and you will see that there have always been catastrophes of one sort or another, but the people have pulled through and that is what you will have to do, for one day you will be part of history that is looked back upon by those of the future and that is all that you will be, just a few pages in the history books for people to say "how dreadful for them" and then go on to something else that interests them at that time!!

Life does go on! But only if you are prepared to let it, you have to play your part in the evolution of your planet, it needs taking care of, if you wish to continue to think of it as your home!!! We feel that this is where we will bid you farewell. We are helping you, believe that both physically and Spiritually. And please know that your loved ones are being cared for by our dedicated bands of helpers, the nurses, the doctors and all of those who minister to the Spirit's that find themselves prematurely upon our plane and wonder what has happened to them. We give them love and it is through that love that they are healed and can continue with their new life and will be here waiting for you when it is your time to depart form this earth plane. You have not lost them, its just that they have gone on ahead of you and you will be reunited with them, for believe that, for we speak the truth to you.

Farewell dear earth friends Farewell and to you Brother scribe we bid you Farewell till next we meet. Farewell.

Chapter 52

YOUTH DOES HAVE A FUTURE

January 31st 2005

There are so many thoughts milling around in peoples heads these days and they begin to wonder just what is happening to not only them but to the World in general. The weather has become somewhat unpredictable, there are catastrophes that happen with no apparent reason as to why they should. The older generations say to themselves "It never used to be like this, I can't understand it"!! The young ones seem to accept what is happening and get on with their lives as best they can, they live for today and as for the future?! Well they can't see that far ahead and so most of them ignore it!! And who can blame them? Because the older generations haven't really given the younger ones anything really positive for them to aspire to!!

And yet, a lot of those younger folk want to know, they want to feel that there is a purpose to their lives, that there must be a future that they can look forward to and not this blank canvas that seems to stare them in the face!! But does anyone tell them that their real future lies not upon this earth plane, but upon the one that so many people call the "Spirit World". But just saying that that is what awaits them when this earth life ends, and not trying to enlighten them further, probably makes them wonder does anybody really know or do people just make things up, hoping against hope that somewhere there's some truth in what they think and say!!! Well that's not good enough for today's youth, they want proof, or at least something that to them makes sense!! They question all the old ideas and quite often come to the conclusion that they are no longer relevant in today's society!! And if the older generations are honest, they will admit that when they were young they felt just the same as the young ones of today feel and think!!

Nothing changes does it? Each generation seeks answers to what this life upon earth really means and they feel they haven't received the answers they were looking for! Yet it they stop and think, they will discover that they have had some of those questions that vexed them answered!! The world has moved on, for each successive generation discovers just a little more of what they call the truth. We are approaching The New Age, one that combines the physical with the Spiritual! So called mysteries will be explained so that they no longer are mysteries, for they have become realities. And with this opening up of the psychic senses they (the youth of today and tomorrow) they will be more receptive to what is sometimes called the "occult world" which unfortunately that word "occult" does not mean what so many people attribute to it! Occult is just another word for Spirit and even the word Spirit makes some people apprehensive! It shouldn't, for that is just what we really are, SPIRIT! This physical body is what the spirit you has been loaned, as it were for the lifetime of that physical unit! When death overtakes the human body it is the "Spirit" that goes on living for the spirit never dies it changes but it is always the you that you know as you!! As spirit we are part of what is termed as "The Creator", another word for "God" if you like, but now is the time for those young people to re-evaluate what they have been told regarding the Creation and not only the one Creator, but what that word really signifies the Creator is an aspect, one aspect, and that means that there are more than one aspect, there are many and all coming under the heading of God!! We, upon this earth and the Spirit spheres that are part of it, even if to earth mans eyes they are invisible! We and that is all of us belong to OUR GOD and always have been, other worlds have their own Gods, and yet all of these God's are aspects of the ONE that is unknowable and always will be. Yet that one allows the humanities on all spheres of existence to view "Him" through those aspect s of "Him" that we call God! And the word "Him" is only an earth word because we cannot possibly envisage what that ONE is really like. For if we were to say The Unknowable One is the Primordial matter of perpetual Life Force! You would have no idea what we are talking about would you? And even we are in awe of that subject!! So you must accept the limitations of our Mind substance that has not been allowed that hidden knowledge and for a very good reason if you care to think about it!!!

We spoke of the New Age which will herald the new thinking of those who belong to it. That is not to say that all that has gone before will be cast aside, it will be viewed with a new perception and shall we say be built upon!! So that future generations will understand far more about the complexities of Creation and those that Create! And the reason why creation is what it is!! Creation is the life force of those Creators who are in turn the very life force of the One who they are aspects of!!!

This discourse is primarily for the younger ones to show them that the Future does exist for them and not only on what you call Planet Earth! And we leave you to think that one out. We say to the little scribe Thank you for your mind transference which you were unaware of until just now!!! And to all of those who we call brethren of the earth we bid you all Farewell till next we meet in thought! Via your little scribe!! Farewell little friend Farewell!

Chapter 53

THE AFTER LIFE IS A REALITY

February 2nd 2005

THOUGHTS NOT MINE!!!

Why is it that we seem to want to glamorise what we call "The Spirit World". It is because we have become somewhat dissatisfied with our life upon earth and the thought that the next one might well be almost a continuation of the one we leave behind? And that to some people would seem like another "life sentence"!! Then to others who have enjoyed their life upon earth the prospect of a continuation of it seems most attractive to them. So what then is the true reality of this one that we gravitate to when we leave the earth body behind?

There are books, articles in magazines, even television programmes, and all of them purporting to know the answers to that question what is the "after life" really like!!? So many conflicting ideas, that its no wonder people are confused and think to themselves "No one" really knows, and to some sceptics they think that there is "No answer"! because when you die that's the end of it as far as they are concerned! And in a way they are quite right! But for all the wrong reasons!!

Granted when the mortal body comes to the end of its life span then it really is the End for that one. With the life force expended from its body it cannot survive as a living entity! So the sceptics can then say, "well I told you so, that's the end of it isn't it? And you really cannot disagree with them on that point, but it is only one point isn't it? They the sceptics do not take into account what or who it was that kept that life force in action while the mortal body was living its life! But then they probably do not even recognise that such a thing as a spirit actually exists! Though just because someone doesn't believe, it does not mean that what they don't believe does NOT exist!! They seem to have blinkered eyes and think that what they cannot see just isn't there!!

And yet there are many, many examples upon earth that they take for granted and yes accept and yet they cannot see the origins only the results as it were. Electricity for one, the force of a hurricane for another, the very air they breathe, one could go on and on, we live in a world that is controlled by what could be called invisible forces, and yet they are real otherwise we wouldn't even be here would we?! So why not accept that as a human body we can only observe just a part of what we are made up of!!? And the real part, that is the invisible part, that never dies even when the physical body does, is a reality in every sense of the word, and that reality extends to the very fabric of what is known as the Spirit world!!! Our next sphere of habitation, where a physical body just could not exist because of its dense matter of construction!! And yet that body was a very necessary adjunct to the spirit one, for it allowed the Spirit to function through its association with the physical, learning from this association and yet at the same time teaching that physical part lessons that only the Spirit has access to via its real home of habitation namely the "World of the Spirit" a joint venture that is of benefit to both parties! One without the other is not complete during the life cycle of the mortal body.

So when the Spirit returns to its homeland leaving the mortal body behind, it takes with it the sum total of what this liaison of these two aspects has taught it, that it can now put into practice as it were, now that is can continue with its, shall we say necessary interruption of its previous life. So this sphere or plane of the Spirit has to have many similarities to the earth plane, similarities but not identical to that lower one of dense matter! For the spirit plane is of a higher vibration, the whole plane has what might be termed a "translucent aspect". Some people might even term it as "dream like" and that is just what is seems like to certain people who are not quite accustomed to the reality of this sphere. You notice we say "people" which implies that you still resemble the person you have been accustomed to being while you inhabited that mortal body that was on loan to you during your habitation upon earth. Though we do stress that your spirit counterpart was able to "come and go" as it were, during this sojourn upon earth! But there is more to that than just those few words imply, which deals with your shall we say "religious convictions" and how they have shaped your inner character! We will not delve any further into that aspect of your life for this writing is for all forms of Religious culture and not just one!! For contrary to what you may have thought All Religions of the earth plane are practised and tolerated in the world of the Spirit, and with this form of toleration, much is learnt and therefore understood and shall we say "developed" by those interested in those cultures!!!

As some of you are already aware this first plane is one of Thought and how you can apply it to your everyday living, for thought is a very powerful tool when it is properly understood and used! So in a way this is a continuation of your earth life but with the exception, you are now free of the encumbrance of a physical body, so you will enjoy the freedom of movement and thought, you still have much to learn if you warrant it, and if not then you progress at a different pace. So look forward to this life that really does await you, it is not a myth it is a Reality believe that for it is the Truth.

And for those of you who are still uncertain about what awaits you when it is your time to depart this earth, just remember that this parting is inevitable it is the only certain thing in life it must end sometime and in that ending a New beginning is beconing you, one to which is no stranger to you, for you have been upon the realm of the Spirit many times before and will no doubt be again.

And so we will bid you friends upon the earth, Farewell and the Blessings of those upon High be with you now and in the days to come. Farewell.

And to the little scribe Farewell little friend and thank you for your patience and the loan of your hand with the pen. Farewell.

Chapter 54

QUESTION! QUESTION! AND THEN QUESTION! AGAIN

February 3rd 2005 12.05 a.m.

We greet you once again dear Brother, and so we will begin. You have been told before about some of the varied aspects of our world. Our world of the Spirit!! You must have wondered, and indeed we know you have, you have wondered just where this world of ours is, where does it exist in relation to the one that is called earth, and we should add not only earth!! Does that make you wonder still further? Your earth consists of matter a dense form of matter and it also vibrates as all worlds and planets do, but not all in the same way, you view the Heavens with their myriads of stars and galaxies that appear to go on into infinity, which is exactly what they do, for to all intents and purposes this universe that we all inhabit cannot be judged by your crude "mileage system". Miles in the universe are flexible which no doubt will confuse you, but then you dwell in an area of space where for the sake of argument you more or less measure your brother planets in mileage, because they are relatively near to you, even when you talk of them in millions of miles, but to venture to the perimeter of your universe just cannot be conceived in even millions and millions, and millions, of earth miles!! Those miles cannot be calculated by earth terms. For they expand and contract just as the universe does with its breathing of the life force! That primordial energy that keeps it forever alive and vibrating, just like your human body and incidentally as your spirit essence does as well!!! Vibration in its various degrees is its very life force, without that form of movement there would be No universe, No Worlds, No Planets, No Life!!!

Think upon that dear friend and know that you can never know the complexities of what constitutes the life force of what you see as Creation. And here we are talking in terms of the scientific community little Brother and not of you personally!!! Creation is forever taking place in the vast cosmos and by Creation you can add the words Non creation, which actually means Creation being de-created to make way for even more creative elements of life that can be sustained within the confines of your known universe! Nothing is lost, nothing is wasted, just altered or shall we say "amalgamated", if you follow what we are implying!! So your perception of what you think you can observe needs to be adjusted for what you perceive need not be a reality as you think of as reality!! Nothing in the universe can be taken at face value, you see what you think you see, which is not quite the same as being identifiable as a Reality that is real and not an illusion of what appears to be real!!!

Hence our desire to try and help you to understand, that illusion forms a very large part of true reality and even that need not be what it seems!!! We are sorry if what we have said leaves you wondering just what IS and what is NOT!!! You are not yet in a position mentally to accept all that we impart to you and so you must just take in what you can and leave what you cannot understand for another time!!! We now return to the subject of "miles", which are really hypothetical measurements of "space" and space is notorious for not being what you think it is!!

So to try and judge distance in space can be rather difficult for space has a habit of being somewhat of an illusion when it comes to, try and measure distances shall we say between the earth and other planets. You cannot measure as it were in straight lines because straight though viewed and thought of as straight is fractured, it is bent, it disappears and then reappears and so you cannot take into account the "depth" of the void that has engulfed a portion of space!!! You could say that there are "pot holes" that your scientific instruments do not take into account where measurements are concerned! And these measurements must also take in the "light years" for what you may think you see could well have disappeared from the realm of Reality thousands if not millions of earth years ago!!! Remember illusion is ever present when dealing with space!!! We started this discourse with you wondering about the Spirit world and its relationship with earth and other planets. Vibration is the key to this question. It can be translated into the word "Invisiblization" that means invisible to you úpon earth but not to those whose habitation that planet of vibrationary force is!! All planets and worlds in fact all that exists in space has a vibrationary force that keeps it in its orbital belt! The higher the vibration the less visible it becomes to those of lower vibrations! Which of course includes the earth plane!!

Your Spirit World comes into the category of the Higher Vibration that is why to you on the earth it is invisible and yet it is a Reality believe that for we; know, we dwell upon one of its many spheres!! Your world is in an Orbital belt and does not move out of it. All planets and worlds dwell within their predestined orbital belts, though sometimes a rogue element escapes form its belt and wanders into another one causing havoc and devastation!! Our and your Spirit realms are in their own orbital belt which is invisible to those on earth and are therefore not affected by any variations that affect that sphere. For our orbital belts, are protected from any outside influences. Even though those belts are in communication with the more gross matter ones. These "belts" are in a way like a vast streams of liquid vapour like substance of High velocity electrical discharge, life force, in fact! That keeps each world or planet in its allotted space, and within, but not of this space belt our invisible worlds or spheres of what you know of as the ones of Spirit dwell, and yes to a certain extent move about for they are not governed by the normal laws of the physical universe! Though they are subject to their own laws of gravitational pull, which are flexible and can be manoeuvred if needed!!!

All this must seem difficult for you go grasp, these laws and belts, and streams of vapour, it must sound a little like "science fiction" but there is more fact in those stories of outer space than perhaps is realized!! Let us just say that we, that is our world's do exist, we are real and not imaginary as you will one day find out for yourself, though you do know about this don't you little friend? These things do not come as a surprise to you, for you do come and go even if you are not always aware of your journeys of the Spirit!!! Remember, in one of your "dream states"? you saw that smaller world travelling along side of the one you were on and then it shot off in another direction, you were viewing what was invisible normally, but for a brief span you could see the invisible made to your eyes visible!!

As we have said, you just cannot be sure all of the time what is fact and what is a form of illusion. One of the lesson's that you will need to learn and put into practice even before you return once more to your home upon the Spirit plane!! And we say to those friends upon the earth plane accept what to you seems feasible and what at this stage you perhaps cannot accept, put it aside and come back to it at a later date and by then it may make more sense to you. Always remember you do not have to take our word for what is said and written. Use your own mind and come to your own conclusions, and that really goes for everything doesn't it? You are not expected to agree with everything that is told to you. You have a brain and a mind of your own, use it, for that is what it is for, question, question, question, that's the only way you are going to get answers that will help you in your searching for the truth and the why we are here, and where we are ultimately going to!!!

And so we will bid you Farewell friends upon the earth plane, and remember Think for Yourselves for nothing is written in stone as you say today. Farewell.

And to you little scribe Farewell and God be with you Farewell, Farewell, till next we meet!

Chapter 55

DISCIPLINE YOURSELF WHEN YOUNG

February 4th 2005

We greet you little Brother in love and understanding. "Life and Death" two of the most thoughtful words that you can come across. For with one there is the expectation of life to be lived, while the other signifies the end of that period of earth life, and yet it is not the end but the new beginning of a fuller life of expectancy!!! Which if you did but know it makes the previous earth one almost pale into insignificance! To most people that statement wouldn't be very convincing taken at "face value". For they understand the reality of life upon the earth plane, for they are the one's who are living it! But the Spirit one! Well that does need thinking about, and yes explaining, with an explanation that stand's up to scrutiny, but "who" can be the one that can do the explaining with an authority that carries conviction?

Most people will say "well that's what the Church is supposed to do isn't it? And in all honesty do you really think that they make a very good job of explaining, what to some seems almost unexplainable by today's standards!! At one time the general population accepted what was told them by the clergy, they had no reason to doubt what was being given to them, and if by chance there were some who voiced dissent at what they were told, they would be labelled "Heretic" and treated harshly. And not only by the Church Authorities!! So most of the dissenters did their dissenting in the privacy of their own homes, or with those of a like mind who they could trust!!!

But today is different! People are almost encouraged to question what for centuries has been almost sacrosanct, for with today's open scientific explanations of the origin's of the universe and even of Mankind himself, soon people will know about the Planet that they are inhabiting and so they will then turn their attentions to what lies beyond this earth when it is time for them to vacate it. In fact for the past hundred years or so the World of the Spirit has been more than just a passing fascination for what many call "The After Life"!! Those scientific bodies talk about E.S.P. and even alien life forms that may or may not exist out there in space and if they do, what can we upon earth do about them!! To some people, they feel their Governments are hiding facts from them and that make's them even more dubious about what those Governments try to explain, they feel that they are not being told all the facts, and that leaves them wide open for misinterpretation of the meagre explanations that are fed to them!!!

Upon your television screens you are given shall we say "glimpses" of what the producers of programmes give to you in the form of "drama's" that really are only for entertainment and very rarely of serious consideration. It whet's the appetite of those who are viewing and they very often seriously want to know more about the life that awaits them when this one is finished!!

That is, those people who are thinking seriously, and are determined to pursue their searching for not only answers but one's that are of the Truth!! The older generations are mostly set in their way's of thinking and so are not likely to be influenced by an Hypothesis that cannot be verified. So it is going to be left to the younger generations of thinkers to pursue what to many is the venture into the unknown!

Yet that unknown, has always been there, even before this so called known existence upon the earth, of Man in his infancy, when Creation was being formed! For it is the Spirit side of Man that was created first and the human side of his character was shall we say almost a bi-product, that allows the Spirit to become attached to the Mortal body for it's life span that is to enable the Spirit to learn lessons that it can only learn by "being" human! And that means to incarnate in a physical vehicle of its "choice"!!

Young minds of today are open to this challenge of Here and the Hereafter. That is when they have learnt the art of personal discipline. At present they do not wish to give up this so called freedom from the restraint of their elders, they forget that one day that title will be theirs and a new younger generation will replace them! But if they do discipline their desires for freedom and learn to cultivate their minds and the thoughts that come from them, they will be in a position where they can be on equal terms with that younger generation that follows them. Not as the older and younger generations of today, where the age gap is a form of hindrance to mutual understanding!!!

So the answer to these youthful explorers of life and what lies beyond, it to study with an open mind, don't dismiss everything of the past, for it is the past that has created the present, and it is up to them to see that their present creates a future of understanding and yes tolerance of others ideals. When the mind is young and impressionable that is when they should be taught about the world of the Spirit and those who dwell upon it, as they will again one day. By which you can understand that first and foremost we are primarily Spirit. That is where we belong, upon the plane of that name and where we return to, to resume our interrupted life upon that sphere of learning when our brief sojourn upon earth is over.

Remember, Spirit a rather loose term for what we really are, but no matter, it is what has become the accepted term for our being of light, just remember that is who we really are, we are part of the Creator of all life. Just a part, but a very necessary part to the Creative Genius who many people call God. You came from that Creator and to that Creator you must eventually return, as Spirit!!! With all of the knowledge that you have accumulated during your many incarnations of learning. Accept your Spirit as part of you, just as the Spirit accepts you the mortal body as part of it!!! We will end our talk here, even though there is much that we would like to tell you but we are told, that that must wait for another time and so we will bid you Farewell dear earth friends and to you little scribe, this has been a surprise discourse for you to use your pen hand has is not? And so we bid you Farewell little friend and know that All is Well for that is true. Farewell.

Chapter 56

REALITY AND PHANTASY WHICH IS WHICH? AND WHICH ONE IS TRUE?

February 13th 2005 3.00 a.m.

A journey of the Mind that takes in Reality and Illusion that will set you thinking!!!

The universe that this world of ours inhabits is one of Material substance, Physical material, and yet it also houses what is loosely termed worlds or spheres of the Spirit! Now to most people the word "Spirit" immediately conjures up thoughts of Non physical beings, some would say that only exist in the imagination, they cannot be what is termed realities! That is not only the "being" but also the sphere to which they supposedly belong. But they are completely wrong in their thinking. For "Spirit" is far more real and yes we say physical than ever the accepted version of "physical", is usually associated with, and what is thought of as the body of Mortal flesh!

"Mortal" which also signifies "Mortality" which in its turn means that what is termed "Mortal" does not last in terms of what is called Eternal! That is the prerogative of the so called Spirit body. So which one would you call the Spirit? The one you are told is that part of the human body that cannot be seen, or for arguments sake the body you accept as Mortal? We know which one we think of as Spirit and it is not US!! And yet Man cannot come to terms with the fact that it is "he" who is the so called Spirit and not the one usually associated with that name! This requires positive re-thinking on his part, but we do not think He is yet ready in his mind to accept this reversal of the roles that have for so long been the accepted version of Reality and Non Reality!!

Now take that a step further and apply that thought to the Universe in general, and then another forward step and think in terms of your world and those planets that you observe in space, that to you upon earth are thought of as realities of the physical!! Because you can see them, but you see only what you expect to see which is quite different from what might exist along side of those seen planets, stars, and cosmic so called debris and what have you!! What you as yet cannot observe are the invisible realities that do actually exist and not just in the mind of one called the observer!! So you see the universe is not only made of substance that could be loosely termed as matter but that matter cannot always be observed for it is forever undergoing change, it disappears only to re-appear in another guise! Now that to US is what we would term as Spirit for it is not, shall we say a permanent form of structure!

We, and the worlds to which we belong and inhabit are the true and lasting realities, even though you upon the earth plane perhaps cannot physically see us in that light! Because we can be visible and then again be invisible! Rather confusing put like that, but that is our form of Reality whereas your life form that is you the mortal being do cease to exist when it is time for your transition to Our plane and that is your Spirit whose life is one of continuity!! Not like your mortal one we are sorry to say!! So just what is reality and what is not? We say that it appears to us that it is your physical world of existence that is the one of non-reality for worlds and their satellites come and go, what you think you can see are quite often not realy there any more, you are seeing what is just an imprint upon the fabric of the universal body, almost like a faded photograph that will one day be no longer observed as to what it was, when once it was part of the living cosmos!!! So much of what you think you see in space is almost an "illusion". The stars, the comets the meteors, realities that disappear when they leave their orbits, their orbit's of imagined reality!! Or perhaps we should have said Your imagined reality which turns out to be just al illusion of the senses!!! It may seem confusing with all this talk of illusion and reality, but in actual fact there are many of you upon your planet that can accept what has been said!! Though to some it may seem like a hypothetical visit into the realms of pure fantasy!! While to others they are realities that they have not dared to voice for fear of ridicule for they are ahead of their time!! Such is progress!! Just try and remember that because you cannot see something, does not mean that it does not exist! It may not in your dimension but in its own it is very much a visible reality and one upon which there exists populations just as real as those upon your earth sphere!!! Which to them, those others your earth and its inhabitants could well appear to be, what you call Spirits!! Just think about that for awhile and you may find that your conclusions upsets all your previous thought's upon the subject!!!

We know we are real as you are too little brother scribe, for your other self, that you know of but as yet cannot see only "feel" is the real and permanent you that exists within and yet without of this "physical" vehicle you call your body, the one that you know will one day no longer exist as a viable entity of habitation!! and the one that can be termed as real goes on living and learning on our and your sphere of permanent structure which is just one of many that await your entry when the time is right in your upward progress that will take you back to the source of all Creation where illusion becomes reality and reality becomes Eternity!!

We leave you on that note of finality dear friends upon the earth plane. You have much to ponder upon after this nights discourse and so we bid you Farewell.

And to you dear Brother we bid you a most fond Farewell from all of those who have contributed to this nights venture into the realms of true reality that may seem at first to be ones of pure fantasy!!! Farewell dear friend Farewell!

Chapter 57

CHANGE YOUR WAY'S OR ELSE!!?

February 17th 2005 1.45 a.m.

Wake up little Brother and here we speak metaphorically for we know you are physically awake!! We speak not of the body but of the thoughts that are generated by the mind that resides within that body! And when we say "wake up little Brother" we could be speaking to all of those upon the earth plane that you call your Brothers!!

So what is it that we mean by "wake up?" It is your inner consciousness, in fact the inner consciousness, of the world at large!! A very large order! You will say, and we agree with you. But that inner consciousness sometimes needs a "jar" to awaken it from it's slumbering! And that "jar! Is often administered by what you call Nature!! That is when she is intent on making her position clear to those upon this dense planet of heavy matter!! And you wonder just what do we mean by that?! You can say when a series of catastrophic events take place upon and within this earth of yours! These so called events" are Nature's way of trying to bring back a form of "stability" to this planet, for too long now Man has been abusing Nature in such a way that the retaliation on her part can only be termed Natural!! You put forward all sorts of theories regarding the change in the weather patterns and what you say is only a part of the true change that is taking place! There is far more than you can ever realize! For deep within the earth there lurks a monster itching to escape from its prison it is the very "life force" of this planet that seeks an outlet of this tremendous build up of "unnatural force" that if it does not allow itself to erupt will turn inward upon itself and then you would see or rather "feel" the disintegration of the very core of this earth of yours, and such devastation would ensue that has not been seen since your earth was originally formed from the Primordial chaos from which it came from!

And so we say to you all Wake Up! Wake Up! Before it is too late! And that means Stop this "deforestation" of your Planet for the forest's are your natural protection from wind and Rain and Fire!! All elements that when "untamed" result in those catastrophic events that we have spoken of!! You have recently witnessed the awful power of not only Fire from under the oceans bed but the sea's that surround your land masses!! Learn from these lessons that are being thrust upon your unsuspecting populations! Your Nations must get together and work out plans that will save this planet of yours from future awful destruction!!! If you do not then this world will be altered almost out of all recognition and as for the populations that dwell upon it they will be decimated!!! Take heed of what we are telling you. Cease this tampering with the Ocean's floor, you are weakening it and causing great splits in its fabric that cannot be mended! That also goes for the atmosphere that surrounds your earth, stop pumping up those gaseous substances that are causing what you call the Green House syndrome!! Do you want to be burnt to a cinder by the strength of your life giving Sun? for you will be unless you put a halt to this deadly pollution!! You are living upon a time bomb, so what are you going to do about it? Wait for it to "go off" or start to re-adjust your planets equilibrium by stopping this senseless rape of your natural resources. You don't replace what you take out and so you are laying yourselves open to all sorts of disasters and yes "diseases" for they quickly follow when a disaster occurs!! You do have the technology, but you use it for all the wrong reasons and that is usually for "greed and profit" two serpents that eat away at the very heart of your society!!!

Take a long hard look at yourselves, you might not like what you see, but if you are willing to change your life style's there is still hope that you can come out of all this turmoil, but you must start NOW, do not leave it till later, for later may came sooner than you think!! And then what will your future generations make of the mess that you are leaving them! That is if there will be any future generations to speak of!! So once again we say Wake Up to your responsibilities, look after your Planet. Study its Needs and work with Nature, and not against her. But it will mean sacrifice and discipline if you are to achieve any lasting results. You have No choice in the matter, either you learn to live in Harmony or die in despair!!!

What will be your answer? We can only hope and pray that you will come to your senses and fast, for time is running out as far as you are concerned and we do not like what we can see might be the outcome if you sit back and be complacent about what we have told you this night!

We will bid you Farewell which on this occasion sounds very hollow to us!! And to you little Brother we bid you Farewell and none of this applies to you!! Farewell!!

Chapter 58

THE AKASHIC RECORDS!

February 18th 2005 12.05 a.m.

A nighttime's discourse with a difference!!!

We take you on a journey little Brother, a journey of the mind! Yours and Ours! Are you ready to proceed? Then let this journey begin. First we take you to where the records called the Akashic Records are to be found. Books of wisdom that were formed even before this your planet of earth was conceived. Records that tell of Planets, Worlds, Universes, of untold variety. As were and still are the inhabitants of those very Planets some of which have long since disappeared, no not destroyed, amalgamated is the word we will use, amalgamated to form even greater Planets, that no longer use this Your Universe as their habitation. For they have since advanced to where they form the Nucleus of even larger and more complex universe's that will one day overtake this one that you inhabit!!

The Records tell of ages past, glorious ages where harmony reigned, where beings of pure light dwelt. Beings of such beauty of form and grace that if you could behold them you would be in awe of what you see!! Your universe is one of many, some are just in the embryonic stage, waiting and sleeping until their sleep state is awakened to a new beginning!! But we do not propose to inform you of those, either past present or future!

We deal with this, your own universe and no other in this

discourse of the mind!! We will tell you of the heavens and the "bodies" you call planets and worlds that circle around their allotted orbits of space. Their programmed passages that they must not venture from. We now proceed to the Temples wherein those records are kept that pertain to this universe. We see many "beings of light" perusing through these vast tomes of History in the making and of History that is past, and yes of History yet to come!!! We as it were circle high above these archives until we are "told" that this is the place of learning that we are looking for. We then descend to one of the many libraries that deal with the various aspects of life within this universe. We are interested in the one that deals with what you call the "Heavens". This building is one of gigantic proportions, with large areas of open space, that is floor space for we are to be shown the Map's of the Heavens that make up various sections of this universe. We search for the Books that will give us the clues that we need to unravel the mysteries of "terrestrial travel". When we find the appropriate book that shows us where we are to find the Map of the Heavens of this universe and also the Key to this knowledge and the word Key does not mean Key that unlocks a door, this Key is the secret Key that will show us the hidden pathways that criss-cross the space wherein dwell all of the life forms of Creation, and here we are speaking of the Planets and their Satellites, the Moons, the Suns, the Stars, and not the inhabitants at this stage of our quest!!!

WE are taken to one of these vast areas and here we proceed to unravel the Maps that when placed together form the whole of the territory that you know of as Space. These Maps are in sections and cover the whole of the floor space that has been allotted for this purpose!! Around this building or what might be called the walls of the inner section of it runs a very long balcony or corridor which almost disappears into the distance, for this gallery is truly vast in it's construction. We ascend to this balcony, or rather we float up to it, for there is no staircase to it!! From our vantage point we can view the panoramic spectacle of the Heavens that are laid out upon the floor.

We can see as it were upon what now appears to us a flat universe with all of it's planets worlds, stars, in fact everything that exists in the Space that we normally view in the round. We are given what seems like a pair of glasses which when we put them on we see in three dimensional form, what we would see from our earth plane when we gaze into Space with our telescopic lenses! These glasses not only magnify but somehow "take in" vast areas of what we are looking at, we see as it were 360 degrees that are stretched out in an elongated fashion, almost like an elastic band of vision! These glasses also let us see beneath the surface as it were of the space that we are looking at, and we can see that there are hidden "pathways" that form almost a "grid like pattern" that covers the whole of the "Space" that makes up the Universal area of our known Universe!!

We "float" over the part of the Space we are observing and as we do we can see that these secret pathways lead to various galaxies and planets and worlds that we have had no knowledge of before this vision that we are viewing!! We can even study these worlds if we wish by re-focusing our spectacles by touching them in a particular way. With these spectacles the maps that we are looking at become three-dimensional and not the flat appearance that they are without the aid of these glasses!! We can "travel" as it were to the utmost limits of our universe without hardly moving from our position!! We are as it were looking down and into the Space and we can see so much that is hidden from view when looking up into Space from our Planet earth. The pathway's that we can see with these glasses are intersected by smaller ones which would allow a traveller or traveller's to deviate from the main pathway and so explore other Planets in other orbits and then if they wish return to the main thoroughfare to continue with their expedition of discovery. But to be able to do all of this exploration they would need a map like the one we are looking at, but on a smaller scale which would "come up" on a screen in the vehicle that they are using to transport them to their intended planet of exploration!

They would be able to plot their course by studying the "grid pattern" of the particular area that appeals to them and then "lock on" to the appropriate hidden pathway that would take them to their destination of choice!!! With our ability to float over this vast map area we can cover in a moment what would take years of movement in the reality of Space travel as it is known upon earth at present!

There is so much more that we would like to show you but we have been informed by the guides who are looking after us on this venture that we must not delve any further into this subject if we are passing on this information to one who dwells upon earth at present. That one being you little Brother!

When it is your time to be with us upon the Spirit realm then you will be able to view in depth all of the Histories that you wish to study past, present, and future! That is all that pertains to this your Universe!!!

The Akashic records are only allowed to be read and studied by those who have been vetted as to their suitability and their ability to understand what they are studying. So it has been a great privilege for us and you dear friend to have been vouchsafed just a glimpse of what Creation is all about! Just a glimpse and nothing more at present!!! Of other worlds of other planets of another time in the life of this Universe of ours!!!

We now bring you back to the reality of this your world of existence. Think about what you have been told and shown this night and pass on this knowledge to those who you feel could benefit from this discourse!

Farewell Brother Scribe till next we meet in Thought transference. Return to your place of slumber, your journey is now over. We bid you a fond Farewell and Peace we leave with you little friend. Farewell.

Chapter 59

CREATOR OR CREATOR'S?

February 19th 2005

THOUGHTS

I put forward a hypothetical question! Do you equate the Creator with what or rather who you understand as your God? By which you will no doubt think that I somehow do not! And so I will not blame you if you decide not to proceed any further with reading what I am about to write!! We and here I'm speaking of all those of the Christian religion, are brought up with this idea of a Father like Deity that we call by the name of God, though there are other Holy names that are applied to "Him" by various religious groups. But what do we really know about the One the Christians call God/ Some say "Our Father in Heaven" a most pleasing reference to associate with the unknown Deity. You will probably say "But He isn't unknown His Son Jesus spoke of My Father and Yours in Heaven". So that surely does imply that God must be of a somewhat Human like figure doesn't it? But are we right to think of God as a human like figure? For the Scriptures say that God made Heaven and Earth in six days and rested on the seventh. Also that when He looked upon His creation which it seems was shrouded in darkness He stretched forth his hand and said "Let there be Light". And there was!! Now if you are going to treat all that was written as actual fact, Can you really and honestly go on thinking that God is like a human like figure and even if He was, surely He would have to be of gigantic proportions if He was responsible for all that has been accepted as His Creation!! And here we haven't even talked about all of the other "creations" that go to make up a world of actual habitation, such as Man and Woman, the beasts of the field, the fowls of the air, the fish of the sea. The trees of the forest and the flowers that add beauty to the landscape. In fact every living thing, visible or invisible. Just pause and think and then think again, and then go into the silence of your inner consciousness and perhaps you will find an answer, though it may not be the answer that you hoped for!!

What was thought of as sacrosanct in times gone by, can now be talked about and discussed openly without fear of being thought of as an heretic and then burnt at the stake, as if that was ever an answer to what a person thought, with that God given gift of an enquiring Mind!!!

You see I do think of God I haven't dismissed Him out of hand have I? I'm trying in my poor way to make sense of things that are so difficult to really understand in this day and age of Enlightenment. We have perhaps got to try and think in a positive fashion and not just accept what we are told by dare I say it? "The Church" in it's broadest sense, and here I'm including not just the Western idea's about God but perhaps some of those of Eastern or Mid Eastern origins!! And I mean No disrespect to any form of Religion however it is practiced!! But to me God seems above all of those previous notions of what "He" is supposed to be like. I feel that some of those artists of the past have a lot to answer for in their portrayals of what they imagine the Creator must look like in human terms! For to me God that is Our God just cannot be visualized in that way. He must be beyond our feeble attempts at trying to explain the unexplainable!

And yet!! I believe "He" has allowed us, his creations, to see Him in our minds as we individually wish to see Him, for I'm sure no two people see God in the same light. They like to feel that "He" is personal in some way to them, especially when they call upon Him as "Father"!!! I too say "Father" in my form of prayer, and yet I do not visualize Him in those human terms. Thinking about it I think I "see" Him as like a "cloud" a vaporous substance that is full of energy and movement and colour that obscures what is within it!! I expect that sounds very peculiar to some, but I feel that just to know that God exists it quite enough for me I don't really have to actually "see" Him and yet I "feel" I am known to "Him"!!!! As indeed we all are!!!

Well now going back to the beginning of this shall I say "narrative"? You will think, "well he seems to believe in God, and yet he says God to him is not the overall Creator so what does he mean by that I wonder"!!! I see the Creator of, how can I put it? The universe or rather Universe's even though we can't see them! Well that Creator is what I would call the Supreme Creator and even "He" is not one but 3 in1! Plus Twelve other Creators of equal standing to each other but not to the three in one!!! These twelve could be called God's in their own right as they are Creators as well!! So you begin to wonder is one of them Our God? Well I don't think so! Our God is the God of this Universe and is the Creator of Our World and all that is in it. We are part of Him as He is part of Us! I feel that He is also responsible, if that is the right word for other worlds and planets that form part of His territory so to speak!! And of course that encompasses many many millions of what we call miles! That forms Space as we know it, or rather as we think we know it!! So taking that a step further. This Universe could be the home so to speak of perhaps a number of Unknown Gods that all form part of this celestial Hierarchy of "Creative Beings" all facets of the ONE SUPREME CREATOR, that will forever be unknown and unseen by humanity in all its various forms!! And that most certainly includes what we like to call our Spirit which is far more of a human being than ever this mortal one can be. For "Spirit", such an inadequate word to describe that essence that comes form God, and that is created by Him, as the part that is the visible part that we know of but cannot "see", only "feel", while we dwell within the mortal body, that is our companion while it, the mortal body resides upon this lower sphere that we call earth!!!

Now if you dear reader have got this far in your reading you will no doubt be ready to give up and say that I probably need my head examining!! You may be right, but there again you may be quite wrong! Whose to say what is right and what perhaps is just maybe!! As none of what I have written can be verified, at least not physically, it perhaps can be in the mind of the one who has done the writing!! But I suppose that really doesn't help you the reader at all does it? So I think that I will cease my writing and retire to my world of the inner thought!!

And so I will bid you farewell and hope that I have given you something to think about that perhaps had not occurred to you before!! Farewell. Farewell, and may the Blessing's of the One on High be with you now and in the day's to come.

"The Little Scribe".

Chapter 60

THE INMORTAL ONE AND ITS MORTAL COMPANION!!

February 27th 2005 2.00 a.m.

THOUGHTS!

I've been thinking and wondering regarding "our Spirit" you would imagine that when the Spirit re-enters the physical world for re-incarnation purpose, as it has done over and over again during its learning periods, it would have at it's disposal literally centuries of information that it has acquired and stored up in that computer like mind. Now with all that information to "tap" into you would think that to be once more upon earth and with a "new" human entity as it's forthcoming companion, it would be in a wonderful position to exert it's authority over this companion. For example steering it clear of any unpleasant circumstances that might cause the physical body much anxiety and even pain!! And looking at it in that light, you would imagine that the physical body would be able to live a fairly stress-free life, in fact a most agreeable one I should think!

But supposing that, that is not the case, and here I'm referring to the Spirits collection of it's past learning abilities that are stored in its Mind substance!! Could it be that when the Spirit is about to begin its "new" incarnation, it's previous memory pattern is shall we say "Put on Hold", just shelved until it returns once more after the conclusion of this incarnation, with it's fresh impressions!! Because if it was allowed access to all it's previous knowledge it would not really be fair on it's mortal companion would it? Because that one would be at a distinct disadvantage in learning how to cope with life, for I'm sure that the all knowing Spirit just could not, as it were "look the other way" if the physical was in some what of a dilemma in a particular situation!!!

If the Spirit and the physical both start off as equals regarding knowledge or the lack of it as the case may be!! Then what they both learn would be relevant in this incarnation and also be what was needed for their progress, both for the physical and the Spirit side of this union!!! Of course that would imply that the Spirit would have been aware of what lessons "it" needed to learn, but not necessarily how it was to go about achieving this!!! So both "parties" would have to rely upon each other for this to have a successful and meaningful outcome!!

When the Spirit returns to it's former habitation and reviews this recent life it has lived upon the earth plane, it would then "release" it's locked up memories of the past and could see how, just what this incarnation has taught it, by coming to it with the fresh approach that has not relied upon it's centuries of knowledge and learning to colour it's outlook!!! Because if it had all that knowledge at it's disposal and was able to use it you would think that it's round of earth incarnations should have ceased long, long ago!!! For lets face it, there surely can't be all that amount of lessons that the Spirit has to learn to equip it for it's journey back to it's source of creation, or can there be? Just what do all these learnt lessons amount to and how can they be justified, that requires the Spirit to need this continual round of incarnations, not only on the earth plane but also on the various spheres of the Spirit World?!!! Surely the lessons that we need for our progress upon the upward spiral, shouldn't require all those "centuries" of trial and error should they? It makes you wonder if there are hidden "handicaps" that prohibit our learning what it is we need to, in our search for the truth of Why we are, what and who we are in our relationship with the Almighty!!! And of course with each other!!! Perhaps there is no simple explanation, and yet I can't see why not, we've been given many examples of how we should and could lead a decent life, one that would be acceptable to God, so why do we find it so hard to do? And here I'm not just talking about our earth life, but also the one of the Spirit, where we should, by rights be in a better position to live a God life as it is intended that we should!!? Are we perhaps, our own worst enemies, when it comes to living an unselfish and God like life?! Is that one lesson so difficult to live by, when we know in our hearts and yes minds that it is the right and proper way to live if we are ever to have the sort of life that God want's us to have, One that would be a fitting tribute to Him, who has given us so much and asks for so little in return?! So perhaps the lesson that we should try and learn is the one of Universal Love for all of our fellow creatures, respect for all of life in all it's aspects and learning not to judge what you do not understand. In other words, just live and let live, and that goes for all the spheres that we may find ourselves dwelling upon as we wend our way back to where we originally came from, The God head, The Creator, the One we call "Our Father". Our God!

And that is where I think I will end my discourse, which I hope will make me think when I read this over when I get up in the morning!!!

Chapter 61

THOUGHT'S ANSWERED

April 13th 2005 1.30 a.m.

In answer to your thoughts dear Brother. We will try to give you an account regarding your Spirit and it's part in the evolutionary progress, and here we stress that when we say "your Spirit" we are talking generally and not necessarily on a personal level!! Though it is to your thought that we are going to give you answers that we hope will satisfy your curiosity!!

Your Spirit, that is the one that functions on the plane nearest to your earth, this one is the one that is responsible for the re-incarnation process that you have been asking questions about. When a Spirit is going to incarnate upon the earth for a specific purpose it has to take into consideration many things prior to it's actual incarnation! You have been told in previous discourse's regarding the Spirit and it's choice of a physical companion for this period. When all of the preliminaries have been properly assessed and the human companion has been decided upon, the Spirit is then ready to embark upon this venture. Now the Spirit then decides upon a strategy which is, that an "aspect" of itself will be the one to which it will be functioning upon the earth plane and not the Spirit original. Do you follow what we are saying?

This aspect which also has an aspect of the Mind substance is now programmed as it were, to become an essential part of the physical body for the incarnation period. Now this "aspect" or rather these aspects are now virtually Newly born Spirit and Mind essence with no previous knowledge of lives past. This is for a purpose, which is that the Spirit in unison with the physical body, now has to "cope" with the coming life cycle for it's learning period. This part or aspect of the Spirit must learn for itself why it is in this position of "living" as it were upon this dense planet. Its prime reason is to learn just as the mortal body is, in overcoming life's problems and in the doing is also character building for both parties!!

Now though this aspect of the original Spirit force is working as it were, on it's own, it does have the Spirit Self, the original one, that knows all that is happening to this aspect of itself shall we say in the "background". But it does not interfere in that ones life style, so that if mistakes are made they must be rectified by the one upon the earth plane, for the freedom of the will extends to not only to the physical but also to it's spirit companion!!

The Spirit is virtually on it's own and must therefore make its own decisions with no help from its original, who until the aspect Spirit returns to its source, when the physical body ceases to function the "original" remains upon the Spirit plane, as shall we say an observer or onlooker, but at the same time it is aware of the life being lived by that aspect of itself and can be in communication with it's Higher selves upon the other spirit planes of existence. If necessary! When the life span of the earth body has reached it's conclusion and the Spirit in released from it and return's to the spirit realm it is that one that has to give account of its activities upon the earth, as you have been told about before. When the Spirit and it's created aspect are ready they are once more joined and become just the "One Spirit" again, with all the knowledge that has been accumulated so enriching the Original spirit via the Mind substance. Now the Spirit can resume it's journey upon this first Spirit plane having fulfilled its mission which has now enabled it to progress further in it's quest for a deeper understanding of the meaning of why it has to undertake these various journeying's on it's way back to the source of it's

Creation. Perhaps this time may even be the last time that it needs these earth incarnations and henceforth all it's future lives will be upon the spheres of the Spirit. We have only been able to give you a very brief idea of just one aspect of a Spirits cycle of lives, but we hope that it has answered some of your unspoken thoughts on the subject. And here is where we feel that we will end this night's discourse. Go on with your thought questions little Brother and we shall endeavour to answer them to the best of our ability!!! We bid you Farewell dear friend and also to those yet unknown to us. Farewell and God's blessings be with you now and in the day's to come.